ROUTLEDGE LIBRARY EDITIONS:
BUSINESS AND ECONOMICS IN ASIA

I0028009

Volume 21

JAPANESE INVESTMENT IN MANCHURIAN MANUFACTURING, MINING, TRANSPORTATION AND COMMUNICATIONS

JAPANESE INVESTMENT IN MANCHURIAN MANUFACTURING, MINING, TRANSPORTATION AND COMMUNICATIONS

1931—1945

ANN RASMUSSEN KINNEY

Routledge
Taylor & Francis Group

LONDON AND NEW YORK

First published in 1982 by Garland Publishing, Inc.

This edition first published in 2019
by Routledge
2 Park Square, Milton Park, Abingdon, Oxon OX14 4RN

and by Routledge
52 Vanderbilt Avenue, New York, NY 10017

Routledge is an imprint of the Taylor & Francis Group, an informa business

© 1982 Ann Rasmussen Kinney

All rights reserved. No part of this book may be reprinted or reproduced or utilised
in any form or by any electronic, mechanical, or other means, now known or
hereafter invented, including photocopying and recording, or in any information
storage or retrieval system, without permission in writing from the publishers.

Trademark notice: Product or corporate names may be trademarks or registered
trademarks, and are used only for identification and explanation without intent to
infringe.

British Library Cataloguing in Publication Data
A catalogue record for this book is available from the British Library

ISBN: 978-1-138-48274-6 (Set)
ISBN: 978-0-429-42825-8 (Set) (ebk)
ISBN: 978-1-138-36911-5 (Volume 21) (hbk)
ISBN: 978-1-138-36914-6 (Volume 21) (pbk)
ISBN: 978-0-429-42886-9 (Volume 21) (ebk)

Publisher's Note
The publisher has gone to great lengths to ensure the quality of this reprint but
points out that some imperfections in the original copies may be apparent.

Disclaimer
The publisher has made every effort to trace copyright holders and would welcome
correspondence from those they have been unable to trace.

Japanese Investment in Manchurian Manufacturing, Mining, Transportation and Communications 1931–1945

Ann Rasmussen Kinney

Garland Publishing, Inc., New York & London
1982

Bibliographical note:
this facsimile has been made from a copy in
the Columbia University Business Library.

Copyright © 1982 by Ann Rasmussen Kinney
All rights reserved

Library of Congress Cataloging in Publication Data

Kinney, Ann Rasmussen.
Japanese investment in Manchurian manufacturing,
mining, transportation, and communications, 1931–1945.

(China during the interregnum, 1911–1949)
Originally presented as the author's thesis (Ph.D.—
Columbia University, 1962) under the title: Investment
in Manchurian manufacturing, mining, transportation,
and communications, 1931–1945.
Bibliography: p.
1. Investments, Japanese—China—Manchuria—History.
2. Investments—China—Manchurian—History.
3. Manchuria China)—Economic conditions.
I. Title. II. Series.
HG5790.M36K56   1982   332.6′7352′0518   80-8835
ISBN 0-8240-4690-0   AACR2

For a complete list of the titles in this series,
see the final pages of this volume.

All volumes in this series are printed on acid-free,
250-year-life paper.

Printed in the United States of America

INVESTMENT IN MANCHURIAN MANUFACTURING,

MINING, TRANSPORTATION AND COMMUNICATIONS, 1931 - 1945

Submitted in partial fulfillment of the
requirements for the degree of Doctor of Philosophy,
in the Faculty of Political Science, Columbia University

Ann Rasmussen Kinney
1962

TABLE OF CONTENTS

		Page
LIST OF TABLES		iii
LIST OF ILLUSTRATIONS		vi
INTRODUCTION		1

Chapter

I. THE SETTING: MANCHURIA, 1930-1945   4

The Consolidation of Power: 1931-1936
The Period of Planned Economy, 1937-1945

II. ESTIMATED INVESTMENT IN CURRENT
PRICES IN MANCHOUKUO INDUSTRY, 1931-
1942   35

Increases in the Paid-up Capital and
Debentures of Corporations in Selected
Manchoukuo Industries, 1931-1942
The Retention of Earnings in Selected
Manchurian Industries, 1930-1942
Financing Manchoukuo Industrial Development
through the Extension of Loans
Total Investment by Component Type Supplied
Annually to Manchoukuo Manufacturing,
Mining, Transportation and Communica-
tions, 1931-1942

III. THE INSTITUTIONS SUPPLYING THE CAPITAL FOR
        MANCHURIAN ECONOMIC DEVELOPMENT   85

        The Routing of Investment Funds to Manchoukuo
          Industry
        Japanese and Manchoukuo Investment in Mining,
          Manufacturing, Transportation and Communica-
          tions, 1932-1944
        The Institutions through which Capital Flowed
          to Manchoukuo Mining, Manufacturing, Trans-
          portation and Communications

  IV. AN EVALUATION OF MANCHURIAN INDUSTRIAL
        INVESTMENT, THE AMOUNT AND ITS SOURCES   124

   V. SUMMARY AND CONCLUSIONS: THE LESSONS OF THE
        MANCHURIAN EXPERIENCE   144

APPENDIX   152

BIBLIOGRAPHY   165

LIST OF TABLES

Table		Page
1.	Plans for Investment in Manchurian Mining, Manufacturing, Transportation and Agriculture as Announced in November 1938	15
2.	Production Targets Set for Industry in Manchurian Economic Plans, 1937-1945	17
3.	Paid-up Capital and Bonds of Manchurian Corporations Engaged in Manufacturing, Mining, Transportation and Communications, 1930-1942	43
4.	Paid-up Capital of Manchurian Manufacturing, Mining, Transportation and Communications and South Manchurian Railroad Holdings of Securities	48
5.	Percentage of Paid-up Capital Accounted for by Transportation/Communications and Mining/Manufacturing in Manchoukuo 1934, 1937, 1942	50
6.	Percentage of Corporate Bonds Accounted for by Transportation/Communications and Mining/Manufacturing in Manchoukuo, 1934, 1937, 1942	51
7.	Sample Study Data on Retained Earnings, Number of Companies Covered, and Paid-up Capitalization	58
8.	Estimated Industry-Wide Retained Earnings in Manchoukuo, 1930-1942	61
9.	Factors Used in Estimating Retained Earnings for 1935 and 1936	63
10.	Estimated Earnings Retained by the South Manchurian Railroad and the Manchurian Telegraph and Telephone Company Prior to 1937	65
11.	Data on Depreciation and the Rate of Depreciation in Selected Manchurian Industries, 1937-1941	69

Table		Page
12.	The Financing of Manchoukuo Manufacturing, Mining, Transportation and Communications through the Extension of Loans, 1932-1945	73
13.	Capital by Component Type Supplied Annually to Manchoukuo Manufacturing, Mining, Transportation and Communications, 1931-1942	78
14.	Recapitulation of Table 20: Capital by Component Type Supplied Annually to Manchoukuo Manufacturing, Mining, Transportation and Communications, 1931-1936, 1937-1941, and 1942	83
15.	The Relative Importance of Different Institutions in Supplying Funds for Manchurian Mining, Manufacturing, Transportation and Communications in 1939	92
16.	Total Investment in Manchurian Mining, Manufacturing, Transportation and Communications and the Relative Share of Japan and Manchoukuo	95
17.	The Channels through Which Japanese Investment in Manchoukuo Mining, Manufacturing, Transportation and Communications Flowed	101
18.	Total Investment Funds for the Four Sectors and the Amount of Funds Available to the South Manchurian Railroad for Investment, 1931-1944	105
19.	Mangyo Investment in Loans to and Shares of Manchurian Subsidiaries, 1938-1944	109
20.	Total Funds Available for Investment and Their Sources, 1931-1941	112
21.	Total Investment in Current and Constant Prices	125
22.	Total Investment in Manchurian Manufacturing, Mining, Transportation and Communications, 1933-1942: In Current Prices, 1933 Prices and 1937 Prices	126

Table		Page

23.   Estimated Annual Increase in the Fixed
Assets of Manchurian Manufacturing,
Mining, Transportation and Communica-
tions, 1938-1942   128

24.   The Estimated Rate of Net Investment in
Manchurian Manufacturing, Mining,
Transportation and Communications for
Selected Years   131

25.   The Manchoukuo National Debt, Treasury
Expenditures and Treasury Receipts,
1932-1945   134

26.   Currency in Circulation, Bank Deposits and
Price Trends in Manchoukuo, 1932-1945   137

27.   Indices for Black Market Prices in Hsinking,
Mukden and Harbin and by Commodity
Group   139

28.   Total Agricultural Production and the Amount
Marketed and Retained for Consumption,
1937-1939, 1940-1942, and 1943-1944   142

LIST OF ILLUSTRATIONS

Figure   Page

1. Production Indices for Planned Goods and
    Consumer Goods, 1936-1944 25

2. Paid-up Capital of all Manchurian Corporations
    by Industry, Adjusted for the Security
    Holdings of the South Manchurian Railroad,
    1930-1942 49

3. Debentures of all Manchurian Corporations by
    Industry 52

4. The Increase in Paid-up Capital and Bonds in
    Manchurian Manufacturing Industries, 1934-
    1942 54

5. The Ratio of Profits to Shareholders' Equity in
    Manchurian Industries, 1937-1942 67

6. Total Annual Increase in Capital Available to
    Manchurian Mining, Manufacturing, Trans-
    portation and Communications, 1931-1942 80

7. Capital Components Available to Manchurian
    Mining, Manufacturing, Transportation and
    Communications, 1931-1942 81

8. The Routing of Capital to Manchoukuo Industry
    1939 87

9. Total Investment in Manchurian Mining, Manu-
    facturing, Transportation and Communications
    and the Relative Share of Japan and
    Manchoukuo, 1931-1944 99

10. Total Investment Funds for Mining, Manufacturing,
    Transportation and Communications and the
    Investment Funds of the South Manchurian
    Railroad, 1931-1944 107

11. Mangyō Investment and Total Funds Available for
    Investment in Mining, Manufacturing,
    Transportation and Communications, 1931-1943 . 110

INTRODUCTION

Manchuria was for all intents and purposes a puppet state of
Japan from 1931 until the end of the Pacific War in 1945. During this
period, the Japanese undertook to develop the economy of the area to
further strengthen the economic basis of the Japanese Empire. This
period, at least through 1943, witnessed the rapid growth of the economy
under centralized planning and control. Large amounts of statistical and
descriptive material relating to these years, usually termed the Manchoukuo Period after the name of Japan's puppet state, are available to the
researcher with some facility in handling Japanese language materials.
It is difficult to think of a comparable underdeveloped area where such
a profusion of reasonably reliable data covering a fifteen year period
is in existence.

Manchurian investment had to be maintained at a high level if the
goals of the Japanese economic planners were to be attained. The financing of this investment was a major preoccupation of the economic authorities
throughout the period. The capital requirements were to be met from
domestic as well as foreign sources. Given the high rate of planned
investment and the underdeveloped character of the Manchurian economy,
one could not expect substantial amounts of capital to be mobilized
domestically through voluntary savings. Had adequate amounts of foreign
investment been available, the planned rate of investment could have been
sustained without undue difficulty. However, lacking this, the economy

was thrown back on its own resources and had to accept the alternative of either reducing the planned rate of investment or meeting the financial targets spelled out by the higher rate of investment through involuntary savings.

In fact, a high rate of investment prevailed during these years. Since investment in heavy industry, transportation and electricity was an important component in this investment, the financing of industry is the subject chosen for this study. Estimates will be made of actual investment in current monetary units. This reliance on financial data will necessitate the construction of some sort of investment deflator if any idea of real investment is to be obtained.

A great deal of attention will be paid to industrial capital by source and type. The Japanese are usually credited with providing the bulk of investment funds in Manchoukuo. However, substantial amounts were collected within the area itself. Estimates of the amounts provided from domestic sources might throw some light on the amount of investment capital which can be mobilized within low income areas. Data are also presented on investment by component type such as retained earnings, paid-up capital, bonds and bank loans. This breakdown will facilitate the analysis of the relationship between the different investment components on the one hand and economic and institutional factors on the other.

The course of inflation during the period will be traced and its relationship to industrial investment studied. In a low income area such as Manchuria, voluntary savings are generally insufficient to finance the desired level of investment. As a result, the economic authorities in underdeveloped areas often resort to financing of an inflationary nature, such as printing money for the purchase of company bonds by the Government.

Industrial investment was not, however, the only cause of inflation; military expenditures and severe price rises in North China also contributed to inflation in Manchoukuo.

The value of inflationary financing as a source of capital formation has been hotly debated in recent years. The negative arguments which predominate stress the economic distortions and foreign trade problems which arise during the course of inflation. However, in Manchuria inflationary techniques prevailed after 1939. At the same time, substantial increases in productive capacity and production took place. Thus, the Manchurian experience may throw some light on the volume of capital available through inflationary processes, the point up to which inflationary financing can successfully be carried, and the institutional factors necessary to make such a policy effective in increasing real investment. Needless to say, these conclusions should be applied to other underdeveloped areas only after taking account of the peculiarities of the Manchurian economy.

CHAPTER I

THE SETTING: MANCHURIA, 1930-1945

Manchuria covers an area of 460,000 square miles,[1] roughly the size of Texas, New Mexico and Arizona. In 1930, its population was 34,335,000[2] and by 1940 it had grown in 43,234,000.[3] Throughout this period Manchuria was basically an agricultural area. In 1930, the little industry which existed was concentrated in the zones under the administration of the Chinese Eastern Railroad and the South Manchuria Railroad. In South Manchuria Dairen, Mukden and Anshan were important industrially. In North Manchuria, where industry was even less developed, Harbin was the only center.

Most industrial enterprises were engaged in processing agricultural products. A large portion of the oil-mills, flour mills and breweries were operated in the traditional manner though they were becoming

---

[1]South Manchurian Railroad, Third Report on Progress in Manchuria (Dairen, 1932), p. 13. This area comprises the four provinces of Liaoning, Kirin, Heilungchiang, and Jehol. The latter province had not been regarded historically as part of Manchuria.

[2]Ibid., p. 13. The 1930 population figure included Jehol and excluded Kwantung Leased Territory. The 1930 census was crude and under-reporting may have occurred. Francis C. Jones (Manchuria Since 1931, p. 206) estimates that 1930 population was actually between 37 and 38 million instead of the 34 million cited above.

[3]The Manchoukuo Yearbook Co., The Manchoukuo Yearbook, 1942 (Hsinking, 1942), p. 119. The first reasonably accurate census of Manchoukuo population was taken in October 1940. The above figure is taken from this census. Some of the growth in population between 1930 and 1940 was spurious depending on the amount of under-reporting present in the 1930 census.

increasingly mechanized. The bean oil and bean cake industries were the
most important in value of output and provided the most important exports. The more modern industries were foreign owned and included iron
works, match factories, cotton spinning mills, tussah silk factories,
cement factories and timber works. However, the contribution of these
enterprises to total production was negligible.

In 1930, foreign investment in Manchuria totalled 2.265 billion
Japanese yen.[4] Of this amount, Japanese investment accounted for 70%,
Soviet investment for 26% and British and United States investment for
only 3%. The South Manchurian Railroad and the Chinese Eastern Railroad
accounted for the bulk of Japanese and Soviet investment. Most of the
consumers' goods made in Manchuria were produced by small scale domestic
industries owned by Chinese. Foreign sources supplied virtually all manufactures. With the exception of some coal fields operated in conjunction
with the railroad, the mineral resources of the area were barely developed.

After the close of the Russo-Japanese War in 1905, Russia ceded
her railroad and mineral rights in South Manchuria to Japan. Shortly
thereafter, the South Manchurian Railroad was organized to administer the
railroads as well as the railroad zone. The South Manchurian Railroad
had numerous functions with little relation to the normal operations of a
railroad. As administrator of the railroad zone, the Company operated
schools, hospitals, hotels, electric power plants and conducted geological surveys. The Company also maintained the Anshan Iron Works.

---

[4]John R. Stewart, "Foreign Investments in Manchuria," Far Eastern
Survey, IV, No. 11 (June 5, 1935), p. 82.

Although control of the South Manchurian Railroad enabled Japanese interests to dominate the Southern portion of the area, some Japanese felt direct control of all Manchuria was necessary to counter the rise of Chinese nationalism and serve as a buffer against the Soviet Union. Nationalistic elements gave many reasons or rationalizations for resuming Japanese colonial expansion. The acquisition of Manchuria was to solve Japan's economic problems and enhance the country's political prestige abroad.

During the early 1930's, protective tariffs were rising all over the world and weakened the position of Japanese business interests which had maintained that Japan's economic interests were best served through the peaceful expansion of trade. The territorial expansionists reasoned that the acquisition of colonies would ensure the access to raw materials and markets necessary if Japan was to be a world power. The addition of Manchuria and possibly North China to Japan's colonial empire was to ensure Japan's economic self-sufficiency. More specifically, Manchuria was to provide much of the coal and pig iron for Japanese industry, soya bean cake for use as fertilizer and agricultural products to feed Japan's population.

The Japanese Army units stationed in the Kwantung Leased Territory were foremost among those wishing to annex Manchuria. During the fall of 1931, the Kwantung Army engineered a series of incidents which enabled it to consolidate its control over all of Manchuria. Shortly thereafter, the puppet state of Manchoukuo was established with Hsinking as the capital. The economic policies evolved during the Manchoukuo Period can only be understood in relation to the ideas espoused by the "young officer" group in the Japanese Army.[5]

---

[5]For fuller information regarding the ideas of the "young officers" group see: Royal Jules Wald, "The Young Officer Movement in Japan, 1925-1937: Ideology and Actions" (unpublished Ph. D. dissertation, University of California, 1949).

The "young officer" group, largely drawn from rural Japan, was antagonistic toward certain economic interests in Japan, the Zaibatsu in particular. They blamed the pervasive economic interests of these large holding company empires for Japan's economic ills during the depression. They also harbored grandiose plans for Japanese expansion in Asia and feared that the economic and political power of the Zaibatsu would be a deterrent. The "young officers" wanted to erect bureaucratic-militaristic controls over the economy of the Japanese Empire. The State has always played an important economic role in Japan, but the degree of economic control envisaged by the Army far exceeded anything experienced in Japan previously.

This "young officer" group was the controlling element in the Kwantung Army. Once the puppet state was established the way was clear for the application of their program to the development of the economy. The unwillingness of the Kwantung Army to use Zaibatsu assistance increased the difficulty of implementing these plans since the Zaibatsu was the most likely source of investment funds and managerial skills.

The Manchoukuo Era is best understood by breaking it down into two periods: 1931-1936, when the Government was organized, its control extended over the countryside and social overhead projects instituted; and the years after 1937 when the five year plans were inaugurated, economic controls perfected and when the tide of war ran against Japan, severely dislocating the economies of Japan and Manchoukuo.

The Consolidation of Power: 1931-1936

To begin with, the Kwantung Army was preoccupied with the maintenance of internal security. The Army was busy putting down banditry and political unrest. Nevertheless, the organizational framework of the Government was set up. The Kwantung Army formed the apex of the structure

which controlled all aspects of life in Manchoukuo. The Commanding
General of the Kwantung Army was simultaneously the Japanese Ambassador
and the directives he delivered to the Prime Minister of Manchoukuo were
followed without question. The Kwantung Army also strengthened its
hand by appointing Japanese to key positions throughout the new
Manchoukuo civil service. The General Affairs Board, the seat of
authority in the Manchoukuo Government, and its six bureaus were
all headed by Japanese and the vice-ministers and bureau chiefs in
most government ministeries and departments were also Japanese.

The basic economic policies of the new regime were promulgated
in 1933.[6] Though an effort was made to enlist the support of the
local populace and soothe foreign business interests, the implementation
of the new economic policies required the institution of thorough-going
government controls. "Special" and "semi-special" companies[7] were
established to manage key industries. Each of these companies was given
virutally monopolistic powers over its industry. The State contributed
a large portion of the capital paid into all the "special" companies.
Though the State was frequently also active in financing the "semi-
special" companies, there was no set rule. The role of the State in the
operation of these companies exceeded the usual rights of stockholders.
All major decisions made by the management of the "special" companies
required government approval and penalties were meted out for non-
compliance with government directives.

---

[6]"Fundamental Policies for Economic Construction", which were promulgated in March 1933, are quoted in the Manchoukuo Yearbook, 1942, op. cit.,
pp. 165-166.

[7]These companies were called "special" (tokushu) and "semi-special"
(jun-tokushu) to distinguish them from private companies incorporated
under Manchoukuo commercial law. Each "special" company was organized
and operated according to the terms of a specific statute. See pp. 20-21
of this chapter for a fuller description of these companies.

At the time the 1933 program for economic construction was announced, three categories of industry with varying degrees of government control were delineated:[8] industries coming under the management of "special" companies; industries requiring a government permit for operation; and those allowed to operate free of government controls. State control was greatest over heavy industries and the utilization of mineral resources and lightest over consumer goods industries. However, within four years the larger scale consumer goods industries were also brought under government supervision.[9]

During this period when the Manchoukuo government was primarily concerned with the consolidation of its political control over the country, a considerable expansion of social overhead facilities took place. Transportation, communications and urban development were given priority and accomplishments in these fields were substantial. For example, railroad mileage increased from 6,500 kilometers in 1932 to 9,260 kilometers in 1936.[10] Though facilities for the generation of electric power and the production of iron and steel were expanded, the government concentrated on establishing the organization necessary for planned industrialization rather than actually expanding productive capacity.

Accomplishments in currency and finance during this early period were substantial. In 1931, Manchuria had no unified currency system. The four chief Chinese banks in the area issued currency as did the smaller Chinese commercial organizations. At least fifteen different sorts of notes and coins of one hundred thirty-six denominations were

---

[8]South Manchurian Railroad, *Fifth Report on Progress in Manchuria* (Dairen, 1936), p. 99.

[9]The important Industries Control Law (Imperial Ordinance No. 66) promulgated in May of 1937, brought the following industries under the close supervision of the State: arms and arms manufacturing; aircraft; cars; liquid fuel; iron and steel; non-ferrous metals; coal; woolen textiles; cotton spinning; cotton textiles; hemp thread; hemp spinning and weaving; flour milling; beer brewing; sugar refining; tobacco; soda manufacturing; fertilizer; paper pulp; oil milling; cement; matches. See *Manchuokuo Year-book, 1942, op. cit.* pp. 174-177 for provisions of Law.

[10]South Manchurian Railroad, *Sixth Report on Progress in Manchuria* (Dairen, 1939), pp. 110-111.

in circulation.[11] Frequent fluctuations in the value of these currencies hindered the transaction of business and prevented the extension of credit on reasonable terms. Foreign currencies were also used as a means of payment. The Yokohama Specie Bank issued silver yen notes in the area and the Bank of Korea issued the sole legal tender in the Kwantung Leased Territory and the South Manchurian Railroad Zone. In addition, Russian rubles circulated in North Manchuria, particularly in the Harbin area.

After the establishment of Manchoukuo, the Japanese introduced a single currency. A series of currency laws passed in 1932, defined the silver standard yuan as the sole legal Manchoukuo currency in areas where extra-territoriality did not apply. Exchange rates were fixed between the existing Chinese currencies and the new Manchoukuo yuan. During the next few years, the old currencies were gradually retired and by the middle of 1935, 97% of the old Chinese notes had been redeemed.[12]

The Central Bank of Manchou was required to maintain the value of the yuan equal to the price of 23.91 grams of pure silver. Currency stability was to be achieved by controlling the amount in circulation and by transactions in silver and foreign currencies on the Shanghai Exchange. In the summer of 1934 when the United States began to buy silver, the price of silver rose and commodity prices in silver fell. The prices of Manchurian soya bean products had already declined by 42%

---

[11]Francis C. Jones, Manchuria Since 1931 (New York: Oxford University Press, 1949), p. 123. This is the best general survey of the Manchoukuo Period in Japanese or Western languages.

[12]Ibid., p. 126.

between 1929 and 1934[13] due to the worldwide depression. The monetary authorities decided to divorce the yuan from silver in order to stem the decline in soya bean prices. In January 1935, the yuan was valued at approximate parity with the Japanese yen, a managed currency.

After protracted negotiations with the Japanese Ministry of Finance, the yuan was linked to the yen at par in the fall of 1935. Japan agreed to recognize the yuan as the sole legal tender in Manchoukuo but it was not until the end of extra-territoriality and the consequent reversion of the railroad zones to Manchoukuo administration in 1937, that the aim of a completely unified currency was accomplished.

The Manchoukuo authorities also reorganized the banking and credit system during this early period. They established financial institutions at different levels of the economy. Two banks, the Central Bank of Manchou and the Industrial Bank of Manchou stood at the apex of the financial structure. The Central Bank was founded in 1932 with the sole right to issue notes. It acted as a repository for the funds of the State Treasury and local administrative bodies and was charged with control of the money market and the maintenance of currency stability. The activities of the Central Bank of Manchou stabilized financial conditions and encouraged the general use of the yuan. When the Bank of Korea withdrew from the financial field in Manchoukuo, the Central Bank took over its functions as agent for the Bank of Japan. In May 1938, the Bank set up a foreign exchange bureau to manage all foreign exchange and assets held by the Government. The Capital Control Law of late 1938, regulating the financial activities of all enterprise in Manchoukuo, was

---

[13]Minami Manshū Tetsudō (South Manchuria Railway Company), Manshū Keizai Nenpō (Manchou Economic Yearbook), Tokyo, 1938, p. 22.

also administered by the Central Bank. Thus, the Bank was empowered to control all the domestic and foreign financial activities of Manchoukuo.

The Industrial Bank of Manchou was the second special financial organ established by the Manchoukuo authorities. Founded in late 1936 to extend long term credit to industry, it also engaged in commercial banking operations. Of an authorized capital of 30 million yuan, 15 million yuan was paid up; half by the Manchoukuo Government and half by the Bank of Korea. The Industrial Bank was authorized to issue debentures up to fifteen times the paid-up capital and the Government guaranteed the principal and interest payments on debentures issued abroad.

The next tier of financial institutions consisted of a number of foreign and domestic private banks and their branches. The domestic ordinary banks were heavily involved in short term financing. After 1933, all banking and credit institutions in Manchoukuo were gradually brought under effective government supervision. The Banking Law of 1933 stipulated that only banks fulfilling certain conditions and licensed to operate by the Government could function. These requirements eliminated the less sound banks.

Most of the traditional native banks had been active as money changers. With the gradual unification of the currency what had been an extremely profitable operation for them became a thing of the past. The linking of the Manchoukuo yuan and the Japanese yen at parity in November 1935 and the enactment of the Foreign Exchange Control Law the following month dealt the final blow to currency speculation. When extra-territoriality was abolished in 1937, all Japanese and foreign banks active in the area came under the banking laws of Manchoukuo.

The reorganization of currency and financial institutions during the initial years of the Manchoukuo regime is to the credit of the authorities there. The controls on currency and finance made it possible for the Government to embark on industrialisation. The linking of the yuan to the yen at parity marked Manchoukuo's full-scale inclusion in the yen block. The free convertibility of yuan into yen gave Manchoukuo access to the capital market of Japan without many of the foreign exchange problems involved in the repatriation and servicing of foreign investments. However, convertibility could not ensure an adequate flow of producer goods into the area.

The Period of Planned Economy, 1937-1945

Toward the end of 1936, the economic authorities felt the time had come to plan the coordinated development of the economy. They believed that the political stability and the institutional changes achieved, would permit the successful implementation of such a plan. The construction programs carried out by the Government and the recovery of the price for soya beans in 1936 accelerated economic activity throughout the area and encouraged the establishment of consumer goods industries to cater to the quickening demand. In view of these trends one can question the need for more centralised planning and control of the economy. The Kwantung Army, however, equated efficiency with control. The Army felt that private enterprise was wasteful because needless duplication resulted. Even so the particular pattern of economic development desired was not based solely on considerations of efficiency but rather on the economic relationship envisaged between Japan and Manchoukuo. All agreed that the Manchurian economy was to be developed in accordance with Japan's needs but there was room for debate as to the exact form this development would take. The authorities gave priority to the development of the iron, steel and electricity industries and the mining of coal, continued to extend the transportation network and paid little attention to agriculture. However, the tempo of industrialization was geared to the resources available in Japan and Manchoukuo and was to proceed without disrupting the economy as a whole.

The five year plan for the economic development of Manchoukuo was the vehicle for this policy. The five year plan took shape in 1936 and in January 1937, the capital requirements and production goals were announced. However, in the summer of the same year, the Sino-Japanese War began and resulted in a full scale revision of the plan's production and investment goals. Total investment called for in the plan was raised from yen 2,583 million to yen 4,963 million. The goals for transportation, communications and agriculture remained the same while those for mining and manufacturing were greatly increased to put the economy on a war footing. Whereas the original version of the plan allocated 58% of investment to mining and manufacturing, the revised plan allocated 79% for these purposes.[14] The revised goals could be achieved without total disruption of the Manchoukuo economy only if Japan and third countries provided sufficient investment and producer goods.

The prices of some producer goods, steel in particular, rose sharply during 1937 and 1938 and these rises necessitated another major revision of the plan in November 1938. The November 1938 formulation of the plan covered the four years 1938-1941. This formulation of the plan is most useful since annual figures are given. The annual injection of capital was set at yen 858 million in 1938 and was to increase to yen 2,041 million in 1941. After 1940, it became increasingly difficult to obtain producer goods from Germany and Italy. At the same time, Japan was devoting more of her resources to the mobilization of the domestic economy. Consequently, the Manchoukuo authorities had to scale down the production targets of

---

[14] Kokumin Keizai Kenkyū Kyōkai, Kinzoku Kōgyō Chōsakai (National Association for Economic Studies, Metals Survey Unit), Dai-ichiji Manshū Sangyō Gokanen Keikakusho (The First Plan for Manchurian Industrial Development), Tokyo, 1946, pp. 113-116.

TABLE 1

PLANS FOR INVESTMENT IN MANCHURIAN MINING, MANUFACTURING, TRANSPORTATION AND AGRICULTURE AS ANNOUNCED IN NOVEMBER 1938 (unit: yen 1,000)

Industry	1937[a]	1938	1939	1940	1941	TOTAL 1938-1941
MINING & MANUFACTURING	(226,000)	598,097	1,191,420	1,428,773	1,771,983	4,990,273
Chemicals		51,479	160,680	355,222	501,020	1,068,401
Synthetic Oil		45,816	156,185	351,548	497,926	1,051,475
Salt		3,513	4,295	3,674	3,094	14,576
Soda		2,150	200			2,350
Metal & Machinery		385,269	723,628	744,187	926,111	2,779,195
Iron & Steel		290,914	583,133	425,656	311,947	1,611,650
Light Metal		19,476	34,000	53,800	10,874	118,150
Lead & Zinc		6,687	15,163	15,662	8,193	45,705
Copper		3,125	3,680	4,980	820	12,605
Gold		65,067	49,152	64,589	62,277	241,085
Machinery			4,000	7,000	4,000	15,000
R.R. Cars			8,000	10,000	10,000	28,000
Automobiles				67,000	40,000	107,000
Planes				70,000	428,000	500,000
Ammunition			1,500	25,000	50,000	100,000
Electricity		73,644	109,246	174,095	143,779	500,764
Mining		83,205	122,328	80,970	88,727	375,220
Coal		82,855	121,998	80,630	88,147	373,630
Asbestos		350	330	340	580	1,600
Lumber & Wood		4,500	73,538	69,299	111,346	258,683
Lumber			25,955	28,652	28,436	83,093
Pulp		4,500	47,583	40,647	82,860	175,590
Foodstuffs[b]			2,000	5,000	1,000	8,000
TRANSPORTATION & COMMUNICATIONS	(217,000)	150,793	171,104	172,071	152,890	646,858
AGRICULTURE, LIVESTOCK & COLONIZATION	(71,000)	109,238	94,428	109,272	116,071	429,008
GRAND TOTAL	(514,000)	858,128	1,456,952	1,710,116	2,040,944	6,066,139[c]

[a]1937 figures refer to the amount actually invested. Figures not included in total.

[b]Refers to meatpacking only.

[c]Differences due to rounding.

Sources: 1937 : Manshūkoku, Sōmuchō (Manchoukuo General Affairs Board) Manshū Keizai Sankō Shiryō (Manchurian Economic Reference Materials), Hsinking, 1939, p. 50.

1938-1941: Uncatalogued document from the Suitsu Collection at Hitotsubashi University, Tokyo. The data refer to the November 1938 formulation of the plan.

the second five year plan due to begin in 1942. These downward revisions
may also have been applied to goals set for 1941 in the first plan.
Table 2 presents data on the production goals of the first five year
plan and the yearly goals set for 1942 through 1945.

The operation of the planning mechanism in Manchoukuo is obscure
but limited insight into the planning process is obtained by examining
some detailed versions of the plan. In other words one must infer the
planning process from the finished product, the plans. In drawing up
the first five year plan the geological resources of the region were
the prime consideration. Manchurian natural resources were surveyed and
the level of production the planners anticipated could be reached on the
basis of these resources after five years of planned economic growth was
estimated. Current productive capacity was subtracted from planned
capacity and the difference, or amount of planned expansion of capacity
was multiplied by a figure representing the unit cost of installing new
capacity. The sum derived in this manner became the investment goal
for the industry in question.[15]

Investment projected in this way appears never to have been related
to national income, previous annual investment or the availability of
domestic or foreign capital for investment in Manchoukuo. Rudimentary
data on Manchurian national income[16] are available for selected years
after 1937 but they had not been compiled when the first five year plan
was initiated. The authorities could ignore these factors because Japan
was expected to make up the difference between planned investment and

[15]Ibid., p. 54.

[16]See Chapter IV.

TABLE 2: PRODUCTION TARGETS SET FOR INDUSTRY IN MANCHURIAN ECONOMIC PLANS, 1937-1945

(unit: 1,000 metric tons)

Product[b]	1941 Goals[a] in Jan.'37 Plan	1941 Goals in May '38 Plan	1942 Goals[c]	1943 Goals	1944 Goals	1945 Goals
Coal	27,160	35,000	27,500	31,450	35,780	40,230
Electricity (1,000KWH)	1,404,600	2,570,000	321[d]	237	345	296
Iron Ore	7,730	16,000	5,340	6,680	7,440	8,790
Pig Iron	2,530	4,000	1,390	1,660	1,760	1,960
Steel Ingots	2,000	3,160	884	1,184	1,263	1,275
Rolled Steel	1,500	1,500	517	589[e]	606	726
Coal Liquification	800	1,770	n.a.	380[e]	470	530
Shale Oil	800	650				
Pulp	120	400				
Gold (Yuan 1,000)	212,000	304,000				
Chemical Fertilizer		454,000				
Automobiles (units)	4,000	50,000				
Planes (units)	340	5,000				

[a] No distinction is made in the literature between production and capacity with regard to the goals of the five year plans. The author assumes that the planning authorities were thinking in terms of capacity and expected the projected capacity to be fully utilized.

[b] Items involving more than yuan 100 million investment during 1937-1941 according to the May 1938 version of the first five year plan.

[c] The source citing the plan figures for 1942 through 1945 does not specify the date at which the formulation took place. The author has assumed the figures refer to the final version of the plan for each year.

[d] The 1942-1945 figures refer to planned annual increase in 1,000 KWH. The comparable figure for 1937-1941 would be 514,100 KWH on the basis of the May 1938 version of the plan.

[e] The 1943-1945 figures are in hectoliters. The author was unable to convert them to metric tons.

Sources: 1941 Goals: Kokumin Keizai Kenkyū Kyōkai, Kinzoku Kōgyō Chōsakai (National Association for Economic Studies, Metals Industry Survey Unit), op. cit., p. 86.

1942-1945: Northeast China Economic Commission, Economic Encyclopedia of the Northeast, Vol. I-B: Resources and Industry of Northeast China (Mukden, 1947), pp. 150-153.

the amount forthcoming from domestic and third country sources. As long as Japanese resources were available to fill the gap, this reasoning was permissable. But, once the Japanese economy faced the task of full-scale mobilization for war, the Manchoukuo planners were deprived of this "blank check" on Japanese investment funds.

When the second five year plan was implemented, Manchoukuo had to rely more heavily than before on domestic resources. Investment funds from countries other than Japan had not materialized and the demands on the Japanese economy were greater. Due to the necessity of mobilizing greater investment within Manchoukuo and of controlling inflation, the planners adopted a more sophisticated approach in framing the investment goals of the second five year plan. At least during 1944 and 1945, planned investment was related to gross national product and aggregate consumption.[17]

A complicated apparatus was set up to formulate and administer the five year plans. The Board of General Affairs of the Prime Minister's Office was the seat of Manchoukuo Government authority. The Planning Bureau (Kikakusho) of the Board of General Affairs implemented the directives issued by the Kwantung Army. This process involved the detailed planning of important objectives, making the necessary adjustments as time went on and the overall coordination of the various organs implementing the plan. The Planning Bureau was also responsible for mobilizing resources necessary to the fulfillment of planned objectives.[18]

---

[17]Northeast China Economic Commission, Economic Encyclopedia of the Northeast, Vol. XIX: Money and Banking in Northeast China (Mukden, 1948), pp. 164-165.

[18]Yutaka Fujiwara, Manshūkoku Tōsei Keizairon (The Manchoukuo Scheme of Economic Controls), Tokyo: Nihon Hyōronsha, 1942, pp. 104-108.

The Planning Committee (Keikaku Iinkai), an extra-governmental joint committee, also functioned in this sphere. This Committee consisted of Japanese, Manchurian, civilian and military authorities. It was set up in 1938 and was divided into a number of sections covering all facets of planning. The major sections were: foreign exchange; materials; labor; finance and trade; industry; colonial development; prices; land and buildings; and industrial location. There appears to have been a great deal of duplication between the Economic Affairs Section of the Kwantung Army, The Planning Bureau of the General Affairs Board and the Joint Planning Committee. There is little information about the interrelations of these planning units. However, in view of the centralization of controls it is assumed that these organizations formed links in the chain of economic command with the Kwantung Army at the top.

The more detailed administrative functions were handled by relevant government ministries. Reorganizations took place from time to time but at the beginning of 1942 the Ministry of Agriculture was responsible for agriculture, livestock and forestry; the Ministry of Finance and Commerce was responsible for engineering, mining, industry, finance, monopolies and the construction of hydro-electric facilities; and the Ministry of Communications was charged with railroads, transportation and communications in general.[19] Productive enterprises falling within the scope of the economic plans were managed by the South Manchurian Railroad, the Manchuria Heavy Industries Development Company and the various "special" and "semi-special" corporations.

Despite the establishment of a number of "special" companies between

---

[19]The Manchoukuo Yearbook, 1942, op. cit., p. 144.

1932 and 1937,[20] the South Manchurian Railroad remained the most important
economic institution. Even so, the interests of the Railroad were narrowed
down considerably between 1935 and 1939. The Company was relieved of many
of its industrial interests although the Railroad retained sizeable blocks
of investments in some concerns, the Manchoukuo Government took over all
the interests of the Railroad in others. Henceforth, the South Manchurian
Railroad was to concentrate on developing railroad and port facilities.
This divesture laid the foundation for the "special" companies which came
to control all sectors of the economy.

The "special" and "semi-special" companies were no different from
private corporations in organization. They were all equipped with a
board of directors, corporate executives from president downwards and
stockholders. The distinction lay rather in their aims as they were
established for the express purpose of expediting the economic policies
of the Manchoukuo Government. The maximization of profits was ruled out
as a major goal though the companies were free to distribute dividends up
to a prescribed rate. Instead the maximization of production was the
goal towards which all the companies were to strive.

The special statute under which each company operated was the vehicle
of external control by the Government. Though differing in detail, these
statutes assured government regulation of the following aspects of company
activities: 1) business plans and their modification; 2) company rules
and regulations; 3) the disposition of bonuses; 4) the subscription of

---

[20]Northeast China Economic Commission, Economic Encyclopedia of
the Northeast, Vol. I-3: Resources and Industry in Northeast China
(Mukden, 1947), Appendix 6, pp. 126-131.

company shares; 5) decisions concerning mergers and liquidations; 6) the transfer and sale of important assets; 7) partial or complete suspension of important business; 8) the appointment and removal of the chairman of the board, directors and supervisory personnel.[21] Thus, the Government was empowered to veto almost any management decision and since the Government was frequently the majority stockholder, it could often control the internal operations of the enterprise.

At the end of the Manchoukuo Period in 1945, there were thirty-six of these companies. Total investment in "special" companies amounted to 11.1 billion yuan, or 46% of total estimated corporate investment in Manchoukuo. If one includes the forty-one "semi-special" companies with total investment of 2.77 billion yuan, the figure rises to 57%. If one further includes investment in the South Manchurian Railroad and the Manchuria Heavy Industries Development Company, total corporate investment of 18.8 billion yuan or an estimated 77% of all corporate investment in Manchoukuo is accounted for.[22]

With the advent of the first five year plan a greater degree of

---

[21]Ibid., p. 15.

[22]Ibid., p. 20. The statistics on corporate investment presented here must be treated charily. The figures include three items: paid-up capital; loans; and liabilities in yuan. The latter item is nowhere explained. The author believes it refers to corporate bonds but other items could also be included. Furthermore, no reference is given for the original source of the statistics. The "special" and "semi-special" companies included are listed in Appendices 6 and 7 (pp. 126-133). Appendix 6 on "special" companies lists thirty-eight instead of the thirty-six mentioned on page 20 where in the author's judgement, the Manchuria Heavy Industries Development Company (Mangyō) and the Central Bank of Manchou were dropped from the list. The 77% figure excludes the capital item of the Manchuria Heavy Industries Development Company since this amount has already been included in the capital item representing investment in "special" companies.

coordination among the "special" companies became essential. In addition, the economic position of these companies had to be strengthened in every possible way. Many of the "special" companies lacked the economic power and prestige necessary to attract private investment and competent executives. Unless this situation changed, the economic authorities could not fulfill the targets set in the revised plan. Under other circumstances Manchoukuo authorities would have asked the Japanese Zaibatsu for assistance but the lack of trust between the Kwantung Army and the Zaibatsu made this impossible. Instead, the Army turned to the shinkō zaibatsu or the "new zaibatsu" which had come into existence after World War I. The economic interests of the "new zaibatsu" were concentrated in iron, steel, light metals and chemicals. The shares were widely distributed and at that time the shinkō zaibatsu did not have the intimate political connections which the traditional Zaibatsu groups maintained.[23]

The Nissan interests (Nissan Sangyō Kaisha) headed by Aikawa Yoshisuke belonged to the shinkō zaibatsu. In 1936, Aikawa was invited to Manchoukuo to assess the possibilities for industrial development in the region and the role which his economic interests might play. The establishment of the Manchuria Heavy Industries Development Company, better known as Mangyō, was the direct result of this visit. The company was organized in December 1937, with the Nissan interests as its nucleus. Initial capitalization amounted to 450 million yuan, 50% of which was supplied by the Nissan group and the remainder by the Manchoukuo Government in the form of industrial assets. Most of the state controlled industrial enterprises were turned over to Mangyō. Many of the subsidiaries of the South

---

[23]Jones, op. cit., p. 148.

Manchurian Railroad were also put under the jurisdiction of Mangyō.

Mangyō marked the departure from the "one company, one industry" system followed until then by the "special" companies. In effect, Mangyō was a holding company set up to manage the following industries: iron and steel, light metals, automobiles, airplanes and petroleum. It was hoped that the personal prestige of Aikawa and the economic position of the Nissan interests in Japan would attract private capital and competent personnel. Manchoukuo authorities even hoped for the participation of Western, particularly United States interests.

Though Aikawa had considerable latitude in routine management decisions, the articles of incorporation for Mangyō gave final authority to the Manchoukuo Government. Aikawa could not have hoped to impose his will on the military. The Nissan interests participated in the Manchurian venture in hopes of making profit-earning additions to their economic empire. Consequently, the Nissan group must have felt that development in accordance with the policies formulated by the Kwantung Army would be profitable. As Japan expected to maintain political control over Manchoukuo in perpetuity, a business man could expect to recoup outlays and receive profits over an extended period. Business interests in Manchuria anticipated increasing benefits from external economies as the economy developed. In the short run, Japanese entrepreneurs were disposed to accept Government interference in management. During the initial ten years, Mangyō dividends were guaranteed at 6% and the stock-holders were to be protected from fluctuations in the market value of their stock.

Mangyō's establishment almost coincided with the China Incident. The implications of Japanese participation in a total war were hardly considered. Aikawa expected to channel foreign capital into his newly established

industrial complex and counted on Germany and the United States to supply
the required producers goods. Had Manchoukuo had access to the economic
resources of these areas, the five year plan goals as revised after the
outbreak of war with China might have been met. But the outbreak of war
in Europe and the increased tension between Japan and the United States
destroyed these hopes. Instead, the Japanese economy had to shoulder the
combined burden of war mobilization in Japan and the industrialization of
Manchoukuo. The strain of this task was too great for an economy operating
on such a narrow resource base.[24] As Japan became progressively involved
in war, even greater emphasis was placed on the expansion of strategic
industries in Manchoukuo. Any semblance of balanced growth between different sectors of the economy was abandoned in favor of the expansion of the
iron, steel and synthetic oil industries.

The effectiveness of government production policies is shown by the
dispersion of production trends between consumer goods industries and
producer goods industries. According to indices compiled by the Central
Bank of Manchou which are graphed in Figure 1, the production in the planned
or producer goods sector rose steadily from 68 in 1936 to 184 in 1942 and
then levelled off at 178 in 1943 and 1944. By contrast, the consumer goods
index started at 81 in 1936, moved erratically to a peak of 109 in 1941
and thereafter declined steadily to 60 in 1944.

The implications of such emphasis on industry in an under-developed,
predominantly agricultural area, are far reaching. The economy of an underdeveloped region can be divided into the "modern" and the "traditional"

---

[24]The Nissan interests headed by Aikawa would probably have clashed
with the Kwantung Army's policies even had economic development proceeded
smoothly. Disputes between the Nissan group and the Manchoukuo authorities
became frequent and increasingly bitter and in 1942 Aikawa resigned and
returned to Japan.

FIGURE 1

PRODUCTION INDICES FOR PLANNED GOODS AND

CONSUMER GOODS, 1936-1944

Index[1]
Value

Planned Goods: Chemicals
Ceramics
Metals
Machinery
& Tools
Electricity
& Gas
Mining
Lumber &
Wood

Consumer Goods: Foodstuffs
Textiles
Paper
Tobacco

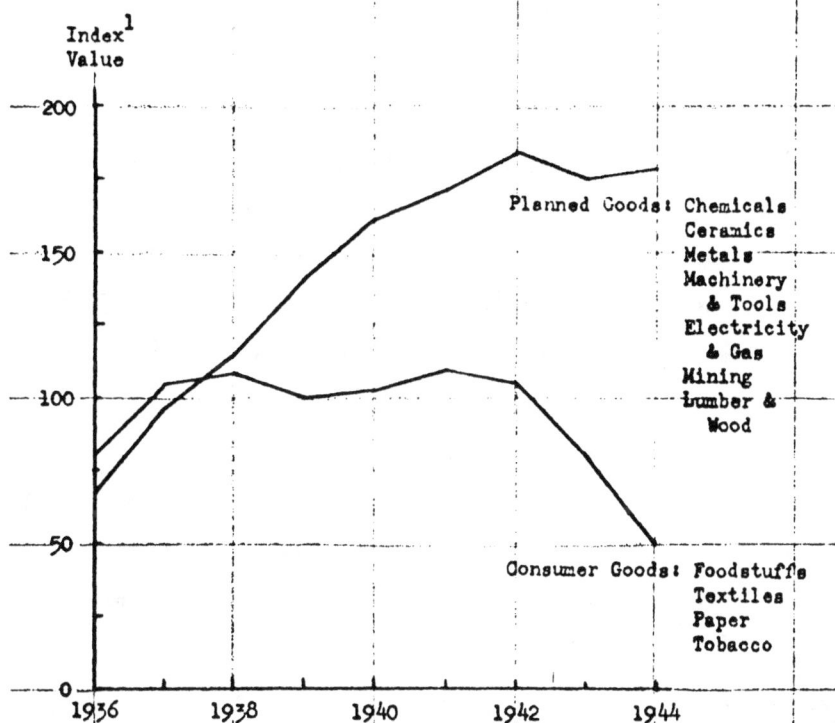

[1]The indices were computed as weighted geometric averages with the 1936-1938 monthly average as the base of 100.

Source: Survey by the Central Bank of Manchou. See Appendix I of this study for a copy of the indices.

sectors. In part, economic activities are classified as "modern" or "traditional" depending on the degree to which modern techniques, such as the specialization of labor, are used. Agriculture in under-developed countries invariably falls into the "traditional" category. Frequently, the agricultural producer strives for self-sufficiency in food and consumer goods. Often his only contact with the market is when surplus produce is sold and consumer goods purchased. Self-sufficiency in agricultural areas results in a compartmentalization between the "traditional" and the "modern" sectors. Since the bulk of economic resources in an underdeveloped country are tied up in agriculture, this compartmentalization greatly complicates the mobilization of domestic resources for economic development outside of agriculture.

In Manchuria the role and character of the agricultural sector differed in important respects. An important segment of Manchurian agriculture produced soya beans and bean products for the world market and had done so for years. The railway network erected by the South Manchurian Railroad opened up the agricultural hinterland and the volume of trade mounted steadily until the depression. In 1930, 5.3 million metric tons[25] of Soya beans were produced and exports of soya beans, bean cake and bean oil accounted for 52%[26] of Manchurian exports by value. The commercialization of agriculture and the growth of processing industries linked rural and urban areas together. Thus, the Manchurian agricultural sector was neither a subsistence economy nor was it isolated from the developing urban areas.

---

[25]South Manchurian Railroad, Fifth Report on Progress in Manchuria, op. cit., p. 164.

[26]South Manchurian Railroad, Third Report on Progress in Manchuria, op. cit., p. 135.

The irony of the situation is that during the Manchoukuo Period, Manchurian agriculture either stood still or retrogressed. During a period when the flow of resources from agriculture to industry and other sectors should have been stepped up as much as possible, everything worked to impede this flow. True, the depression lowered the prices of soya beans but though prices recovered by 1936, soya bean production never reached the 1930 level again during the Manchoukuo Period. The emphasis on heavy industry in the five year plans was a major factor in stemming the flow of resources from agriculture to industry. Consumer goods became scarce and this scarcity robbed the farmer of incentive to produce for a market where agricultural prices were held unduly low by government controls. Actually, the Government did little to encourage the improvement of agricultural techniques for the revised version of the first five year plan viewed the industrial complexes being developed in Manchuria as outposts of the Japanese economy. In fact, the economic authorities inattention to agricultural development forced them to rely more heavily on Japanese resources and later when Japanese assistance was reduced, they faced a dilemma which could not be solved by existing economic controls.

The control over production exercised by the Manchoukuo authorities through the special companies and the Important Industries Control Law was but one form of economic regulation. By the end of 1940, provisions had been made to control the allocation of all factors of production: capital; labor; and raw materials. Prices were gradually brought under supervision by various agencies controlling the collection and distribution of consumer as well as producer goods.

Direct controls on production were limited to industries cited in the five year plans for industrialization. At no time did the Manchoukuo Government attempt to impose state management on agricultural production either because close supervision of the channels of collection and distribution would suffice or because the Government lacked the personnel, popular support or funds for collectivization.[27] Exception might be made for the colonization programs to promote the settlement of large numbers of Japanese and Korean agriculturists in Manchoukuo through Government subsidies. However, the rationale behind colonization was primarily strategic.

In fact the Government was not able to control the level and composition of agricultural production through the agencies for collection and distribution and this lack vastly complicated the development of industry. To the extent that agricultural prices were effectively fixed at levels unfavorable to the farmer, the agriculturists shifted to the production of commodities for household use or to those not effectively controlled. The marketable surplus of basic foodstuffs declined which worsened the lot of the urban dweller and raised the already high rate of labor turnover in industry.[28] The stagnation of agriculture also cut down Manchoukuo foreign exchange receipts from exports particularly of soya bean products and was particularly detrimental as long as producers' goods were obtained through trading with third countries. After the outbreak of war between Germany and the Soviet Union, goods could no longer be routed over the Trans-

---

[27]The author has searched for material on the Japanese attitude towards collectivizing Manchurian agriculture. The only item unearthed was a small monograph published by the South Manchurian Railroad on Soviet collective farms. This study merely presented all available data on Soviet collectivization. The material itself was never related to the Manchoukuo case.

[28]Ramon Meyers, "The Japanese Economic Development of Manchuria" (unpublished Ph.D. dissertation, Department of Economics, University of Washington, 1959), Chapters on agriculture and labor.

Siberian Railroad from Europe to Manchoukuo and trade with third countries became negligible.

Initially, Manchoukuo planning authorities had relied on financial controls in carrying out the five year plan. By the end of 1939, these relatively indirect methods had proved ineffective and were replaced by an elaborate system of issuing allocation permits to high priority enterprises.[29] The Materials Mobilization Plan (Busshi Dōin Keikaku) was announced in 1939 to ensure the allocation of the factors of production in accordance with the goals of the five year plan. Available supplies of raw materials from foreign as well as domestic sources were estimated and allocated according to priority. A similar plan had already been introduced in Japan and the Manchoukuo Materials Mobilization Plan was coordinated with it.

Special companies were set up to administer this system of collection and distribution. The Japan Manchoukuo Trading Company (Nichi Man Shōji Kabushikigaisha) was to supervise all transactions in iron, steel, non-ferrous metals, coal, chemicals, drugs, ammonium sulphate and soda ash. Similar companies administered dealings in light metals, cement, lumber, cars and tires, leather and furs, and linen goods. This system was also extended to the consumer goods sector. The Manchou Agricultural Products Company (Manshū Nōsan Kōsha) was to control the rice, wheat and soya bean trade while the Manchou Daily Necessities Company (Manshū Seikatsu Hitsujuhin K.K.) regulated most consumer goods.[30]

These special companies were to simplify the channels of distribution

---

[29]Northeast China Economic Commission, op. cit., p. 36.

[30]Fujiwara, op. cit., p. 203.

sufficiently to enable the Government to control them. The middleman was
to be eliminated and agricultural products collected by agricultural cooperatives (Konō gassakusha) were passed on to the "special" companies
while the products of the mining and manufacturing sectors were collected
directly from the producing units. The "special" companies imported goods
directly from Japan but made use of import traders in purchases from other
countries. Distribution within Manchoukuo to large consumers such as the
Army or other special companies was handled directly without recourse to
middlemen. Sales of small lots were carried out by retail dealers in
urban areas and by agricultural cooperatives in rural areas. Exports to
Japan were handled by "special" companies dealing directly with the
Japanese purchaser while exports to other countries were handled by
traders.[31]

The Government expected its agencies to dominate domestic wholesale
trade and whenever possible retail trade also. Had this ideal plan worked
out in practice, the Government might have been able to direct economic
flows by manipulating prices and regulating supply and demand more directly
and ensured the smooth functioning of the planned economy. But no sooner
was this scheme outlined and its implementation begun than private whole-
salers and foreign trade firms exerted efforts to nullify it. Firms
importing goods into Manchoukuo from Japan were particularly effective in
this respect. As stated above, the "special" companies were to import all
goods from Japan directly. At this time, approximately 80% of the consumer goods were imported from Japan.[32] But the Government modified its
stand on imports from Japan and allowed the private traders to continue

---

[31]Ibid., p. 208.

[32]Ibid., p. 215.

with the result that it became difficult to ensure the distribution of goods at official prices.

Price controls were gradually and imperfectly inaugurated. Iron and steel products were the first affected. In 1937, the official start of war between China and Japan caused a sharp rise in the prices of these items. Shortly thereafter, iron and steel prices were controlled by the Japan Manchoukuo Trading Company which was in charge of all iron and steel sales. The purchase and sales prices of the various products were set[33] and any positive differential deposited in a balance fund which was to cover losses which might be incurred by a negative differential. In 1938, when the Materials Pricing Committee (Busshi Bukka Iinkai) was organized under the Planning Committee, the pricing and allocation policies were fixed by it and administered by the Japan Manchoukuo Trading Company.[34]

In 1939, two types of prices generally prevailed: official prices which were fixed by the central or provincial government; and control prices which were fixed by "special" or "semi-special" companies and the control associations formed by producers or traders. At that time official prices prevailed in the case of wheat, wheat flour, raw cotton, cotton goods, tobacco, leather and furs. Control prices applied to coal, iron and steel, lumber, cement, seed cotton, rice and cereals. The prices of

---

[33] Price controls on steel were probably similar to those applied to other commodities. Total steel available from domestic and foreign sources was ascertained and the cost of producing domestic and purchasing imported steel was estimated. Total estimated cost was divided by total tonnage available to arrive at an average cost figure which became the government price. See: Northeast China Economic Commission, I-B, op. cit., p. 25.

[34] Fujiwara, op. cit., p. 136.

foodstuffs, drugs, cosmetics and stationery were fixed at the provincial or city level.[35] By the end of the first five year plan, the administrative machinery for the control and coordination of the economy was complete and changes thereafter, were in response to very specific situations.

Whereas the first five year plan for Manchoukuo had been designed as an independent project, the second plan was an integral part of the overall economic plan for Japan, Korea, North China, Mongolia and Sinkiang. After the second plan began in 1942, periodic meetings were held by leaders from these areas to decide the allocation of raw materials and finished products within the economic bloc. They followed the instructions of the Japanese Planning Council and all their decisions were reviewed by the Japanese Economic Advisory Board.[36]

Manchoukuo planning techniques greatly improved during the first plan. The importance of applying a crude input/output type of analysis in relating production goals to each other and to available resources was recognized and prior to the announcement of the second five year plan, available supplies and requirements had been carefully examined. Consequently, the Materials Mobilization Plan and the plans for expanding production and capacity were well coordinated in advance. The drafting of the second five year plan was completed in November 1941. Once again the outbreak of war, this time the bombing of Pearl Harbor, threw off the carefully made calculations. Nevertheless, the plan did serve as a general guide.

[35]Ibid., pp. 204-205.

[36]Northeast China Economic Commission, I-B, op. cit., pp. 50-51.

The economic plans for the yen bloc gave priority to shipbuilding and repair, iron and steel, coal, electricity, oil, machine tools, aluminum and non-ferrous metals. The high priority given to shipbuilding is noteworthy. The activities of American submarines were particularly effective against Japanese shipping after the middle of 1943. Japan's lines of communication between the home islands and the military outposts in the Pacific were gradually cut off. The severe reduction in the amount of merchant shipping available to transport goods to and from Japan in 1944 and 1945 also made the exchange of goods between Japan and Manchoukuo difficult. As United States bombing of Japan's industrial centers was stepped up, the destruction of industrial capacity reduced Japanese requirements for inputs. Since Manchuria was supplying raw materials and semi-finished goods to Japan, this reduction in Japan's demand for industrial inputs reduced the demand for the products of Manchurian industry. In fact, by 1945, the Japanese gave priority to shipping space for the import of foodstuffs rather than industrial materials.[37]

The economic coordination within the yen bloc called for in the second plan strained the transportation system of Manchoukuo. This factor plus the shipping shortage prompted efforts to enable Manchurian industry to produce more finished goods by transferring complete facilities for the processing of steel materials and the production of aircraft from Japan to Manchoukuo. Since these steps were taken in 1945, there was no time to implement this policy.

The continuous decline in Japanese economic assistance to Manchoukuo plus the increasing emphasis on a narrow range of strategic goods generated

---

[37]Jerome B. Cohen, Japan's Economy in War and Reconstruction, University of Minnesota Press, 1949, p. 371.

strong inflationary pressures within the economy. The hoarding of goods and black market activities increased. The police attempted to move against these activities but by the end of 1944, pricing and distribution controls had so broken down that the "authorities were actually directed to use black market channels."[38] The Manchoukuo Government and the Kwantung Army assigned people to purchase raw materials on the black market for export to Japan and domestic use.

During the last year and a half of the war, the administrative apparatus and the productive resources of Manchuria proved inadequate to cope with the wartime economic problems. The Government increasingly resorted to ad hoc emergency measures in dealing with situations as they arose, but to no avail for conditions deteriorated steadily.

---

[38]Northeast China Economic Commission, I-B, op. cit., p. 53.

CHAPTER II

ESTIMATED INVESTMENT IN CURRENT PRICES IN MANCHOUKUO
INDUSTRY, 1931-1942

The investment targets set in the five year plans were ambitious and
the need to fulfill these targets motivated many of the institutional
developments during the Manchoukuo Period. The Japanese and Manchoukuo
authorities were more concerned with raising the level of investment in
Manchurian manufacturing, mining, transportation and communications than
with any other program or policy instituted during the period. The level
to which investment increased and the methods used to raise and maintain
a high level of investment are the central themes of this study.

The purpose of this chapter is to estimate the total amount of capital
available in current prices for investment in Manchurian mining, manufacturing, transportation and communications. It is impossible to evaluate
the success of the economic authorities in attaining the goals of the
five year plans until such an estimate is made. It is also impossible to
judge the relative effectiveness of different methods of financing investment without an estimate of total investment.

Total capital available for investment in these Manchurian industries
has been estimated by summing up annual increases in paid-up capital,
bonds, loans and the amount of earnings retained. These four components
will account for most financial investment. Estimates of financial
investment frequently diverge from those of investment based on a commodity flow type of analysis. Double counting, the problems of aggre-
gating data during a period of rising prices and the use of capital

collected for non-investment purposes are among the serious defects of estimates based on financial investment. But in view of statistical materials available, this method was the only one open to the author.

Fortunately, there are certain advantages to using series on financial investment. For one thing, it is easier to locate the source of investment when using a money flow type of analysis because at the initial stage, investment is made in the form of money and only later are the funds transformed into producer goods, construction or inventories. Furthermore, paid-up capital, bonds, loans and retained earnings, the components of financial investment, represent methods of financing as well. The relative weight of the four investment components depends greatly on the importance of the government and private sectors, business practices and price trends.

In the case of an economy effectively controlled by the government, the distinction may break down completely and investment components may be such good substitutes for each other that they are indistinguishable in effect. For example, in investing a portion of government revenues in a government controlled enterprise, the choice between the purchase of stock or corporate bonds may be based on little more than bookkeeping considerations. Once the central economic authority has selected the industry and the firms which are to receive the funds, the actual form taken by the investment can be academic. Nevertheless, the distinction of investment by component type is still useful in analyzing the methods and institutions employed in fulfilling the economic plans.

The time series presented in this chapter show beyond doubt the great growth of industrial investment during the Manchoukuo Period. Total annual investment in Manchurian manufacturing, mining, transportation

and communications, in current prices, ranged from yen 320 million to
yen 366 million during 1934-1936, the years just prior to the first
five year plan.[1] Annual investment roughly doubled rising to yen 600
million during 1937 and 1938 and a peak of yen 1,780 million was reached
in 1939. Thereafter, annual investment levelled off at yen 1,750 million
in 1940, dipped to yen 1,215 million in 1941 and rose again to yen 1,640
million in 1942, the last year for which complete data are available.
These figures show a tremendous growth of investment in current prices
but if the series is deflated by the equipment goods price index compiled
by the Central Bank of Manchou, investment during the period is reduced
by one-third.

This study of industrial finance[2] is restricted to metals and machinery, ceramics,[3] chemicals, lumber and wood products, electricity and gas,
mining, transportation and communications, the industries to which the
Government channelled capital. For comparative purposes data are also
presented on two consumer goods industries, textiles and foodstuffs.
The latter industries were not given priority by the Government and their
inclusion in this study can indicate the degree of government influence

---

[1]See Table 13 for data in current prices and Table 22 for the
investment series as deflated by the equipment goods price index.

[2]The organizational types of businesses included were determined by
the availability of data. Global data referring to the number of companies
and their paid-up capital are broken down into three categories: incorporated businesses (kabushikigaisha); limited partnerships (gōshigaisha);
and unlimited partnerships (gōmeigaisha). At the end of 1941, the paid-up
capital of all these concerns amounted to yen 5.123 billion of which
incorporated businesses accounted for yen 4.899 billion and limited and
unlimited partnerships the remaining yen 0.229 billion /These figures are
taken from Manshū Chūō Ginkō (Central Bank of Manchou), Jūnenshi (Ten
Year History), Appendix 17/. Thus, non-incorporated businesses accounted
for less than 5% of total enterprise capital. About half of the capitalization of non-incorporated businesses was devoted to trading which is
outside this study. It is safe to assume, therefore, that the exclusion
of partnerships will have little effect on the results.

[3]Includes cement, dolomite and talc.

on the direction and volume of investment.

Data relating to the planned sector for the years from 1937 through 1941 are extensive. Since not all manufacturing industries were designated as planned industries, data are more readily available for some industries than for others. Thus, there are more materials dealing with the iron and steel industry than with, for example, textiles or foodstuffs. Descriptive and statistical studies covering the 1931-1936 period do not concentrate on any particular group of industries. Statistical data which lend themselves to time series analysis are difficult to obtain for these early years.

Japanese language sources referring to the period after 1941 are difficult to locate. In the early 1940's, the flow of materials from Manchoukuo to Japan dried up so there is little available in Japanese libraries. The collection of documents and books built up within the area by the Manchoukuo Government and the South Manchurian Railroad are lost to Western scholars for the time being. This means that in some instances it is not possible to carry the analysis through the end of the Manchoukuo period in 1945. Only the initial ten or eleven years of the Manchoukuo period can be studied in detail and the years begin with a depression and end with global war. The brevity of the time span plus the two above named exogenous factors require caution in using the crude time series presented in this chapter.

Section 1. Increases in the Paid-up Capital and Debentures of Corporations in Selected Manchoukuo Industries, 1931-1942.

Statistics on the amount of paid-up capital and bonds of Manchurian corporations are available in several of the statistical yearbooks published during the period. Unfortunately, annual totals given by different

publications differ and no one series is available for the whole period.
The two criteria used in selecting data were the greatest probable global
coverage and comparability with the statistics of other years. Through
1938, the South Manchurian Railroad data meet both these criteria[4] so
Railroad data were selected for these years.[5] There was little choice
of data for 1939. Statistics compiled by the Railroad cover only the
first six months of the year and Manchoukuo Government publications omit
the bulk of bonds outstanding in the transportation sector. Consequently,
two publications have been used to supplement each other, the compilations
of the Economic Affairs Section of the Manchoukuo Government[6] providing
most of the data on paid-up capital and the South Manchurian Railroad
series those on corporate bonds. Another publication of the South Manchurian
Railroad is used for the years 1940-1942.[7] Global data covering the sectors

---

[4]In fact, prior to 1938, the South Manchurian Railroad was responsible for most of the economic research done on Manchuria as well as
the compilation of statistical series. The Dairen Chamber of Commerce
also published a great deal but the research efforts of this organization
were much inferior to those of the South Manchurian Railroad.

[5]These statistics are available in two South Manchurian Railroad
publications:
a) Manshū Keizai Nenpō (Manchou Economic Yearbook)
b) Manshū Keizai Tōkei Nenpō (Yearbook of Manchou Economic Statistics)
   The figures in the former publication are more aggregated as manufacturing is combined. There are occasional differences in the totals
presented in the two publications but the discrepancy is often so small
it could be due to differences in rounding.

[6]Manshūkoku, Keizaibu (Manchoukuo, Department of Economic Affairs),
Manshū Keizai Tōkei Geppō (Monthly of Manchou Economic Statistics), Hsinking, March 1940.

[7]Minami Manshū Tetsudō (South Manchuria Railway Company), Manshū
Keizai Tōkei Kihō (Quarterly of Manchou Economic Statistics), No. 1
(Nov., 1941), No. 3 (Sept., 1943).

selected for study are not available for the last two and a half years
of the Manchoukuo Period.

Statistics on corporate capitalization and debentures prior to 1934
are given only in aggregate. The capitalization of individual industries
during 1930-1933 is estimated on the assumption that the relative importance of each industry during these years was similar to that of 1934.
The industrial structure was reasonably stable prior to 1934 as the
greatest impetus to Manchurian industrial development came after 1936/1937.[8]
This method assumed that all industries grew at an equal rate during 1930-
1933.

At the end of 1935, the first year for which statistics are available
on corporate debentures by industry, all but yen 1.4 million of the yen
687 million of total debentures were accounted for by mining, manufacturing, transportation and communications.[9] Since the amount outside the
sectors included in this study was so small, it is assumed that all bonds
outstanding prior to 1935 belonged to the four study sectors.

The presence of firms containing substantial vertical integration

---

[8]However, the modern sector of the Manchurian economy was very small
in the early 1930's. Consequently, the entry of one large firm into an
industry could noticeably influence its relative importance in the economic
structure. From the establishment of Manchoukuo until the end of 1934,
the Government organized ten "special" companies (See South Manchurian
Railroad, Fifth Report on Progress..., Appendix p. 1.) and three of these,
the Manchuria Telephone and Telegraph Company, the Manchuria Coal Mining
Company and the Manchuria Electric Company were large enough to exert an
influence on the capital structure of the modern sector of the economy.
However, these three firms were based on the reorganization of existing
firms in whole or in part so the effect of their entry on the industrial
structure is less than their capitalization would indicate.

[9]Minami Manshū Tetsudō (South Manchuria Railway Company), Manshū
Tōkei Nenpō (Yearbook of Manchou Statistics) 1937, Part II, p. 487.

and diversification has clouded the analysis of structural shifts within the sectors under study. All capitalization and bonds of the South Manchurian Railroad are listed under transportation although the Company was engaged in many activities totally unrelated to transportation.[10] In 1935, paid-up capital in the mining industry is given as yen 37.6 million and bonds outstanding as yen 10.45 million. At the same time, the South Manchurian Railroad listed fixed assets in collieries amounting to yen 119.8 million.[11] Coal mining is closely related to the operation of a railroad but the inclusion of the entire South Manchurian Railroad in the transportation statistics means that there is a strong downward bias in those for mining. The Showa Steel Works, another integrated firm has large deposits of iron ore which more properly should have been listed under mining and several enterprises operated thermal power stations which should have been included in the electricity industry.

Were one using the substantive approach in estimating investment in Manchoukuo, the value of these misplaced assets could theoretically be credited to the correct sector.[12] Since the claims approach is being

---

[10]Prior to 1937 when the cessation of extra-territoriality ended the South Manchurian Railroad's administration of the railroad zone, data on the capitalization of the Railroad implicitly include items completely outside the scope of this study.

[11]South Manchurian Railroad, Fifth Report on Progress..., op. cit., Appendix, p. 1.

[12]See: Simon Kuznets, "On the Measurement of National Wealth", Studies in Income and Wealth (New York: National Bureau of Economic Research, 1938), Vol. II, p. 6.
In effect, the substantive approach involves listing all physical assets in an area, giving them a monetary value and then summing up these values. The claim approach is an alternate one. It involves listing all claims held by investors against the physical assets, placing a monetary value on these claims and then totalling these values. The latter approach which is based on the amount of existing equity capital, bonds outstanding and loans, has been used in this study.

used this statistical juggling of assets is not permissable. One can only state that an upward bias exists in the statistics on equity capital in transportation and metals and a corresponding downward bias is present in data for the mining and electricity industries. Fortunately, these misplaced assets within the sectors under study do not affect the amount of total investment.

The existence of the South Manchurian Railroad and Mangyō, enterprises similar to holding companies, introduces the problem of double counting. Every effort has been made to correct for this double counting. Both companies are included in their entirety in the statistical series covering all Manchurian corporations.[13] Since Mangyō itself conducted no productive operations, its capital item and debentures outstanding have been excluded from the figures in Table 3. The investment activities of Mangyō relative to its affiliates are reflected in the changes in paid-up capital and the amounts of debentures outstanding in the accounts of these subsidiaries.[14]

The South Manchurian Railroad cannot be treated as summarily as Mangyō since its role as a producers of goods and provider of services far out-weighed its function as a holding company. Fortunately, data are available

---

[13] Only the South Manchurian Railroad appears in the statistical categories presented in Table 4. Mangyō is always listed in categories such as "Financial" or "Holding Companies".

[14] Unfortunately, the financial relations of the South Manchurian Railroad and Mangyō with their subsidiaries were not limited to holding corporate shares and debentures. Both companies were active in extending loans to subsidiaries and affiliated enterprises. Since the statistics on the volume of loans to various industries cover only the credit activities of banks and other purely financial institutions, this type of enterprise lending activity must be accounted for elsewhere. This problem will be taken up in the section on the amount of funds made available to industry through loans.

TABLE 3: PAID-UP CAPITAL[a] AND BONDS[b] OF MANCHURIAN CORPORATIONS ENGAGED IN MANUFACTURING, MINING, TRANSPORTATION AND COMMUNICATIONS, 1930-1942. (unit: yen 1,000)

		1930	1931	1932	1933	1934	1935	1936	1937	1938	1939	1940	1941	1942
Metals	No.[c]					18	14	16	20	33	41			
	PUC	51,900	51,207	53,338	72,573	83,578	105,648	115,948	147,448	191,302	193,717			
	No.							1	1	1	1			
	Bonds						10,000	28,000	28,000	28,000	76,700			
Machinery & Tools	No.						15	17	32	45	79			
	PUC						10,538	15,022	25,940	59,898	176,105			
Chemicals	No.					36	38	48	58	75	115			
	PUC	19,547	19,286	20,088	27,333	31,830	46,840	71,685	106,225	124,855	717,707			
	No.									1	1			
	Bonds									10,000				
Lumber & Wood	No.					20	20	26	25	30	n.a.			
	PUC	2,696	2,660	2,771	3,770	4,563	6,055	8,190	7,960	9,430	18,311			
Ceramics	No.						34	41	44	51	50			
	PUC	7,117	7,315	7,620	10,368	12,144[d]	17,932	21,190	22,230	27,263	41,584			
Group A	No.											458	574	677
	PUC											1,078,305	1,294,128	1,493,105
	No.												3	3
	Bonds											105,300	127,650	148,250
Textiles	No.					14	21	24	31	33	40			
	PUC	9,436	9,310	9,698	13,195	15,256	16,371	24,138	36,242	49,882	56,427			
	No.						1	1	1	1				
	No.						1,000	1,000	1,000	1,000				
Foodstuffs	No.					37	47	56	71	77	80			
	PUC	13,481	13,300	13,854	18,850	21,390	31,713	42,572	50,324	51,205	56,753			
	No.						1	1	1	1				
	Bonds						1,000	500	500	500				
Miscellaneous[e]	No.					27	30	38	48	55	n.a.			
	PUC	4,044	3,990	4,156	5,655	6,786	11,082	67,645	92,797	98,560	92,607			
Group B	No.											330	449	609
	PUC											324,453	386,592	469,068
	No.											2	2	2
	Bonds											1,500	1,500	1,500

TABLE 3 (continued)

		1930	1931	1932	1933	1934	1935	1936	1937	1938	1939	1940	1941	1942
Electricity & Gas (Group C)	No.					7	19	18	22	18	24	12	13	22
	PUC	79,535	78,472	81,739	111,216	128,515	102,978	103,345	141,530	153,717	157,137	199,064	283,319	291,571
	No.						1	1	1	1	1	1	1	2
	Bonds						10,000	25,000	25,000	24,000	61,600	121,200	179,175	264,900
Total Manufactures	No.						238	284	351	417	n.a.	800	1,036	1,308
	PUC	188,054	185,540	193,264	262,960	304,062	349,157	469,735	630,466	766,112	1,510,348	1,601,822	1,964,033	2,253,744
	No.						3	4	4	5	2	5	6	7
	Bonds						21,000	54,500	54,500	63,500	138,300	228,000	308,325	414,750
Mining	No.						16	16	31	42	61	74	90	102
	PUC	14,829	14,630	15,240	20,735	24,288	37,600	37,825	77,162	160,188	380,515	816,827	1,090,443	1,343,036
	No.						2	2	2	2	1	3	3	2
	Bonds						10,450	10,450	10,450	20,450	39,000	74,450	83,050	94,700
Transportation	No.					31	55	58	67	75	65	101	111	114
	PUC	262,496	263,770	277,654	364,278	413,196	439,220	423,320	578,940	649,036	683,227	742,487	807,293	1,343,159
	No.						4	4	4	4	3	3	4	4
	Bonds						639,100	793,875	813,850	928,437	1,006,612	1,374,905	1,650,160	1,886,015
Communications (1 company)	No.						1	1	1	1	1	1	1	1
	PUC	18,199	17,955	18,703	25,448	29,375	29,375	36,250	36,250	36,250	43,125	55,625	68,125	100,000
	No.						1	1	1	1	1	1	1	1
	Bonds						15,000	15,000	23,000	29,000	41,000	48,850	70,050	91,050
TOTAL FOR FOUR SECTORS	No.					236	310	259	450	535	n.a.	976	1,238	1,525
	PUC	483,577	481,895	504,861	673,421	770,921	855,352	967,130	1,322,818	1,611,586	2,617,215	3,216,761	3,929,894	5,039,939
	No.	4	4			9	10	11	11	12	7	12	14	14
	Bonds	300,977	320,452	393,927	388,950	575,175	685,550	873,825	901,800	1,041,387	1,224,712	1,726,205	2,111,585	2,486,515
TOTAL FOR ALL SECTORS	PUC	580,637	577,659	604,610	809,142	926,101	997,154	1,135,848	1,575,816	1,954,254	2,983,481	3,891,540	4,724,597	5,976,728
	Bonds	300,977	320,452	393,927	388,950	575,175	686,950	875,225	903,200	1,086,781	1,338,105	1,938,198	2,533,553	3,109,758

TABLE 3 (continued)

Differences are due to rounding.

ᵃThe amount of paid-up capital attributed to various industries during 1930 -1933 was estimated on the basis of the relative importance of individual industries in 1934. See the text for justification of this procedure.

ᵇAll bonds outstanding in Manchoukuo during 1930-1934 were ascribed to manufacturing, mining, transportation and communications as a whole. During 1935-1942, bonds are given by industry as listed in the statistical sources. All bonds of the South Manchurian Railroad are included in the transportation sector.

ᶜKey to column headings: No.: Number of companies whose paid-up capital is listed in the sources

PUC: Amount of paid-up capital given for the above number of companies

No.: Number of the above companies with bond issues outstanding

Bonds: Amount of bond issues outstanding

ᵈCeramics and mining were combined in the statistical sources in 1934. The two industries were separated on the basis of their relative importance in 1935. Ceramics was then included in manufacturing to make the coverage of this sector comparable to that in the following years.

ᵉMiscellaneous manufacturing includes such activities as printing, the tobacco and match industries.

ᶠThe statistics for electricity and gas during 1940-1942 refer to Industrial Group C and also include coke and briquette making.

ᵍMining include gold, coal and miscellaneous extractive industries.

ʰAll South Manchurian Railroad liabilities are included in the transportation sector in the statistical sources used for this table. As explained in the text it was found advisable to deduct South Manchurian Railroad holdings of securities in other companies from total paid-up capital in transportation and from the four sector total. Thus, figures cited for transportation in this table differ from the original statistical sources by the amount of South Manchurian security holdings. See Table 4 for data on the amount of securities held by the Railroad and the unadjusted totals.

TABLE 3 (continued)

SOURCES

1. Minami Manshū Tetsudō (South Manchurian Railway Company), Manshū Keizai Tōkei Nempō (Yearbook of Manchou Economic Statistics), Dairen, 1937, No. 2, p. 487.

2. Minami Manshū Tetsudō (South Manchurian Railway Company), Manshū Keizai Nempō (Manchou Economic Year-book), Tokyo: Kaizōsha, 1939, pp. 23-25.

3. Minami Manshū Tetsudō (South Manchurian Railway Company), Manshū Keizai Tōkei Kihō (Quarterly of Manchou Economic Statistics), Hsinking, No. 1 (November 1941), pp. 110-111, and No. 3 (September 1943), pp. 96-97.

4. Manshūkoku, Keizaibu (Manchoukuo, Economic Affairs Section), Manshū Keizai Tōkei Geppō (Monthly of Manchou Economic Statistics), op. cit., March 1940, p. 28

Manufacturing:

1930-1933	Estimated
1934	Source 1
1935-1938	Source 2
1939	Source 4
1940-1942	Source 3

Mining:

1930-1933	Estimated
1934	Source 1
1935-1938	Source 1
1939	Source 4
1940-1942	Source 3

Transportation:

1930-1933	Estimated
1934	Source 1
1935-1938	Source 2
1939	Paid-up capital: Source 4
	Bonds: Source 2 (refers to July 1)
1940-1942	Source 3

Communications:

1930-1933	Estimated
1934-1942	As in Transportation

on the yearly investment totals of the Company in other firms. This investment took the form of holdings of stocks and bonds as well as credit loans.
The investments of the South Manchurian Railroad comprised by stocks and
bonds of other companies have already been counted in the statistics on
paid-up capital and corporate bonds outstanding in the Manchoukuo economy.
In order to avoid double counting, the amount of Railroad holdings of
securities[15] has been deducted from the total amount of paid-up capital of
incorporated businesses in the sectors under study and from the amount of
paid-up capital in the transportation sector. Readers interested in the
magnitude of the adjustment made for Railroad holdings of securities in
other firms and the statistics on paid-up capital as presented in the
original sources are referred to Table 4. Statistics on loans to the
different economic sectors cover only those made by banks so no double
counting has occurred with respect to South Manchurian loan investment in
other companies.[16]

The tremendous growth in the amount of paid-up capital of Manchurian
corporations is illustrated graphically in Figure 2. Transportation and
communications have been combined as have mining and manufacturing. Total
paid-up capital in all Manchoukuo corporations grew from over one half

---

[15]The Railroad held bonds as well as stocks in other companies.
Unfortunately, the two categories are combined in the balance sheets under
the heading of securities. As of August 1945, South Manchurian Railroad
holdings of stock and bonds in other companies totalled yen 505 million.
Of this amount, only yen 2.5 million was in bonds. (See: Ōkurashō (Japanese
Ministry of Finance), Nihonjin Kaigai Katsudō ni Kan suru Rekishiteki Chōsa
(A Historical Investigation of the Overseas Activity of Japanese), Tokyo,
1947, Vol. III of the section dealing with Manchuria, Appendix 7) Since
this amount is inconsequential, the author has assumed that all holdings of
securities consisted of shares.

[16]No data are available on bank loans to transportation though data
are available on loans to other sectors. The author assumed that the South
Manchurian Railroad rather than the banking system served as creditor to
the transportation sector.

TABLE 4

PAID-UP CAPITAL OF MANCHURIAN MANUFACTURING, MINING, TRANSPORTATION AND
COMMUNICATIONS AND SOUTH MANCHURIAN RAILROAD HOLDINGS OF SECURITIES

(unit: yen 1,000)

Paid-up Capital Unadjusted for
South Manchurian R.R. Holdings

	Transportation	Manufacturing Mining Transportation Communications	South Manchurian Railroad Holdings of Securities in Other Companies
1930	355,887	576,968	93,391
1931	351,130	569,255	87,360
1932	365,748	592,955	88,094
1933	497,644	806,787	133,366
1934	573,146	930,871	159,950
1935	639,078	1,055,210	199,858
1936	624,530	1,168,340	201,210
1937	730,945	1,474,823	152,005
1938	766,170	1,728,720	117,134
1939	897,797	2,831,785	214,570
1940	1,000,730	3,475,004	258,243
1941	1,101,396	4,223,997	294,103
1942	1,675,747	5,372,527	332,588

Sources: Paid-up Capital for Manufacturing, Mining, Transportation
and Communications, Sources as given in Table 3.

South Manchurian Railroad Security Holdings: Ōkurashō
(Japanese Ministry of Finance), Nihonjin Kaigai Katsudō ni
Kan suru Rekishiteki Chōsa (A Historical Investigation of
the Overseas Activity of Japanese) op. cit., Appendices 3
and 4.

FIGURE 2

PAID-UP CAPITAL OF ALL MANCHURIAN

CORPORATIONS BY INDUSTRY, ADJUSTED FOR THE

SECURITY HOLDINGS OF THE SOUTH MANCHURIAN RAILROAD, 1930-1942

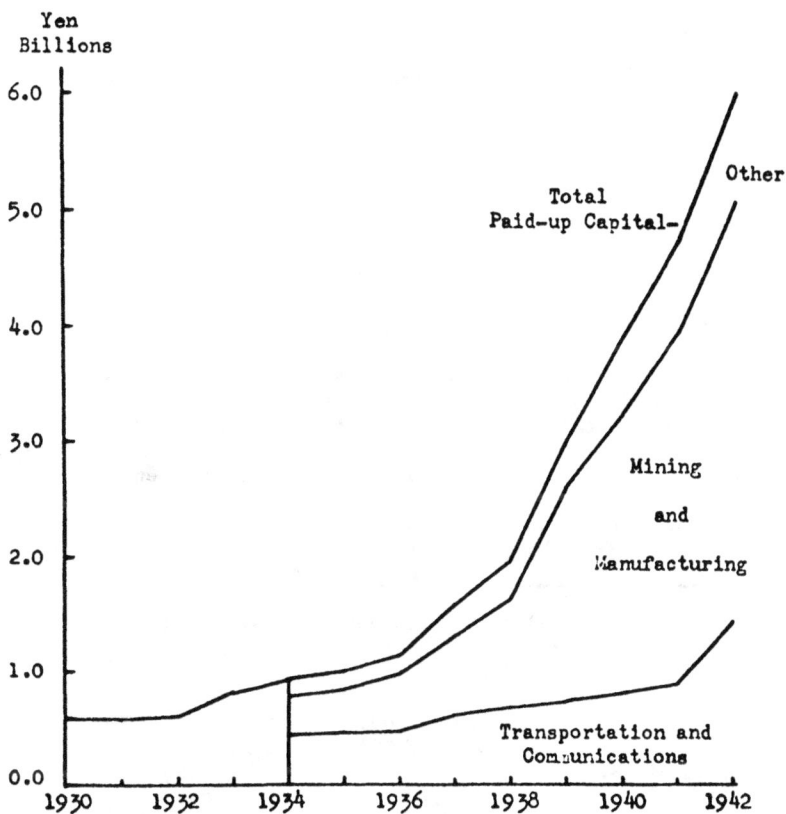

The curves are cumulative

Source: As in Table 13

billion yen in 1930 to six billion yen in 1942.[17] The changes in the composition of paid-up capital by economic activity are shown in Table 5.

TABLE 5

PERCENTAGE OF PAID-UP CAPITAL ACCOUNTED FOR BY TRANSPORTATION-COMMUNICATIONS AND MINING-MANUFACTURING IN MANCHOUKUO, 1934, 1937, 1942.

	1934	1937	1942
Transportation- Communications	48%	39%	24%
Mining-Manufacturing	35%	45%	60%
Other	17%	16%	16%
TOTAL	100%	100%	100%

Sources: As in Table 3.

The relative importance of transportation and communications measured by paid-up capital declined steadily throughout the period while that of mining and manufacturing increased correspondingly and the share of other sectors remained the same. The establishment of Mangyō as a holding company for the mining and manufacturing sectors was responsible for most of this shift. Mangyō holdings of shares in mining and manufacturing enterprises rose from zero in 1937 to yen 1,892 million[18] at the end of 1942

---

[17]Total paid-up capital for all Manchurian corporations less South Manchurian Railroad holdings of securities and excluding the paid-up capital and bonds of Mangyō was as follows:

	1930	1942
Paid-up Capital	yen 580,637,000	yen 5,976,728,000
Bonds	300,977,000	3,109,758,000

Source: As in Table 3.

[18]"Heavy Industry in Manchoukuo," Oriental Economist, XII, No. 2 (February 1945), p. 71.
However, not all of this amount represented new investment. The initial capitalization of Mangyō was set at yen 450 million and the Manchoukuo Government was to provide half of this amount. But the Government's contribution consisted largely of shares in existing corporations and thus represented a transfer in the ownership of existing assets rather than net investment. This factor was only important in 1937 and 1938.

and accounted for 65% of the yen 2,890 million increase in the paid-up
capital of these sectors.

Figure 3 plots the rise in the amount of corporate bonds outstanding
from yen 0.3 billion to over yen 3 billion. The preponderance of bonds in
transportation and communications is apparent. In 1935, transportation
and communications accounted for 94% of the total and mining and manufacturing for 5%. Only after 1938 were bonds in "Other" activities substantial
enough to be graphed. By the end of 1942, the share of bonds in the transportation and communications sector had fallen to 64% while those in mining
and manufacturing had risen to 16% of the total. Although the relative
importance of bonds outstanding in transportation and communications declined,
these sectors continued to account for more than half of all bonds.

TABLE 6

PERCENTAGE OF CORPORATE BONDS ACCOUNTED FOR BY TRANSPORTATION-COMMUNICATIONS
AND MINING-MANUFACTURING IN MANCHOUKUO, 1935, 1938, 1942.

	1935	1938	1942
Transportation-Communications	94%	78%	64%
Mining-Manufacturing	5%	13%	16%
Other	1%	9%	20%
TOTAL	100%	100%	100%

Source: As in Table 3.

The financial policies of the South Manchurian Railroad were responsible for the preponderance of bonds in transportation and communications.
The Railroad relied on the flotation of bonds rather than the sale of stock
or on bank credit for financing its expansion. The Railroad was well-known
to investors in Japan and Manchoukuo who considered it a prime risk and the
Company's bond issues were readily absorbed by the capital market. No other
company in Manchoukuo was in this enviable position.

FIGURE 3

DEBENTURES OF ALL MANCHURIAN

CORPORATIONS BY INDUSTRY, 1930 - 1942

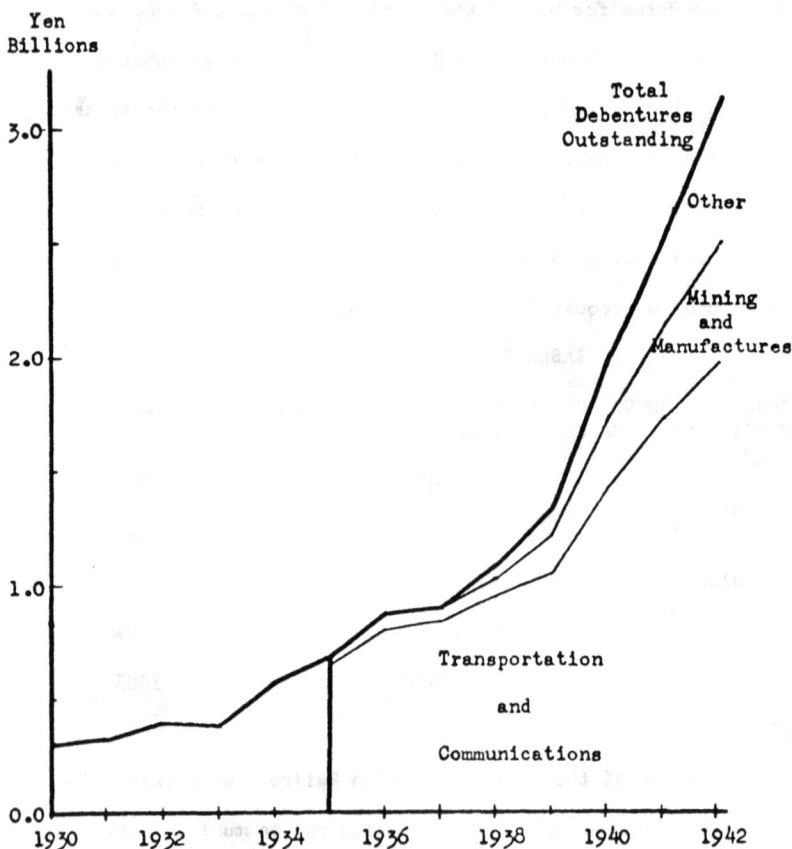

The curves are cumulative.

Sources: As in Table 3

The sub-sector distribution of paid-up capital and bonds in manufacturing is illustrated by Figure 4. The manufacturing sector is divided into groups A, B, and C, comprising respectively heavy industry, light industry and electricity and gas. During 1939, the paid-up capital of Group A increased sharply from yen 412 million to yen 1,148 million. The chemical industry alone provided yen 593 million of the yen 736 million total increase.

The relative importance of bond and share financing varies markedly from group to group. In Group A, bonds amounted to only 10% of paid-up capital while in Group C, electricity and gas, they are roughly equal after 1940. In Group B, light industry, bond issues are negligible and can not be graphed.

Investors normally choose to invest in stock or bonds depending on their estimation of price trends and the prospects and financial policies of the company in question. By 1940, prices were rising sharply while the rate of profit to shareholders' equity was falling in all industries except tobacco so there was little incentive for the private investor to buy bonds or shares, particularly in chemicals, ceramics, metals and machinery, electricity and gas or mining where profit rates were about half of those for textiles, foodstuffs, tobacco, lumber and wood. Therefore, government institutions had to assume the task of investing in Manchoukuo industry and the investment instrument chosen depended upon administrative rather than economic considerations.

Section 2. The Retention of Earnings in Selected Manchurian Industries, 1930-1942.

Retained earnings in selected Manchurian industries have been estimated

FIGURE 4

THE INCREASE IN PAID-UP CAPITAL AND BONDS

IN MANCHURIAN MANUFACTURING INDUSTRIES, 1934 - 1942

Yen
Billions

Corporate Paid-up Capital   Group C

2.0

Group B

1.5

1.0

Group A

0.5

0.0

1934   1936   1938   1940   1942

Yen
Billions

0.5

Corporate Bonds

Group C

Group A

0.0

1934   1936   1938   1940   1942

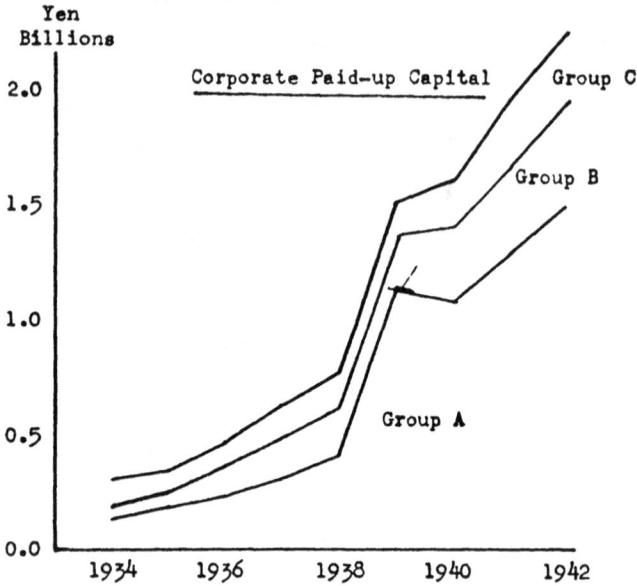

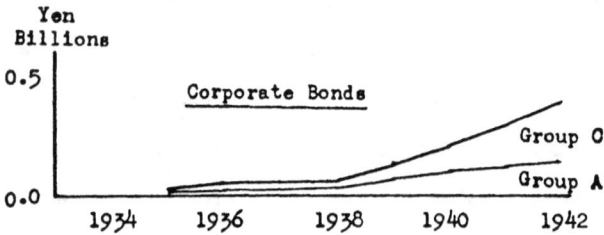

Group A	Group B	Group C
Machinery & Tools, Metals Chemicals Ceramics, Lumber & Wood	Textiles Foodstuffs Miscellaneous	Electricity & Gas

The curves are cumulative.

Sources: As in Table 3

on the basis of three independent studies[19] of corporate finances made

covering various years from 1930 through 1942. The feasibility of linking

---

[19]These studies are as follows:

(a) Minami Manshū Tetsudō (South Manchurian Railway Company) Manshū Kaisha
Kōkahyō Shūsei, Kōgyōhen (Compilation of Records of Manchurian Corporations,
Volume on Manufacturing), Dairen, 1936. This study covers 1930-1934 quite
fully but provides only partial figures for 1935. The study was to com-
prise three volumes dealing with the following sectors: Volume I, Finance
and Trade; Volume II, Manufacturing; and Volume III, Transportation and
Communications. Only the first two volumes are available and the third
may never have been published. This publication is not an analysis of
enterprise finance but a compilation of corporate balance sheets. The
form of the balance sheets seems to have been standardized in the process
of publication though there are differences among the companies in the
frequency and dates of balance sheet publication. The industries covered
by the volume on manufacturing are textiles, foodstuffs, tobacco, chemicals,
ceramics, mining, metals and machinery, electricity and gas, lumber and
wood products. Companies included initially were carried through 1934/
1935 unless they went out of existence. Occasional newly established companies were included during the 1930-1934/5 period.

(b) Dairen Shōkōkaigisho (Dairen Chamber of Commerce), Manshū Jigyō Seiseki
Bunseki (Analysis of Business Results of Manchurian Enterprises), 5 vols.,
Annual 1937-1941, Dairen. This series does not seem to have been published
for the years following 1941. Data have been compiled covering all sectors
of the economy. The statistics presented are based on balance sheet data
which have been considerably reworked by the publisher to facilitate analysis.
Figures are given by company and various profit rates and dividend rates
are computed by company as well as for each industry as a whole.
    The coverage of the Dairen Chamber of Commerce annual is substantially
greater than the publication of the South Manchurian Railroad covering the
earlier years. No adequate explanation is given regarding the criteria
used in deciding whether or not a company should be included. Occasionally
companies which had been in existence for some time are added and others
which continued to function are dropped. The Dairen Chamber of Commerce
Study has been used as the basis for estimating retained earnings from
1937 through 1941.

(c) Manshū Kōgyō Ginkō (Industrial Bank of Manchou), Manshū Jigyō Kaisha
Seiseki Bunseki (Analysis of Business Results of Manchurian Enterprises
and Companies), Annual, 1941-1942, Hsinking.
    The Industrial Bank publication which is parallel to the Dairen Chamber
of Commerce study, is based on more rigorous statistical methodology. In
this study 239 identical firms are covered each year and analyzed separately from enterprises which may have been added or dropped during the period.
Unfortunately, only the 1941 and 1942 volumes are available. The 1941
volume gives summary data for 1939 and 1940 but no breakdown is given for
individual firms. The Industrial Bank of Manchou data was used in estimating retained earnings in 1942.

together estimates of retained earnings based on three separate studies
is open to question. Assessment of the comparability of estimated
retained earnings based on the South Manchurian Railroad publication with
those based on the compilations of the Dairen Chamber of Commerce, in this
study was based on data available for 1934, the last year fully covered
by the South Manchurian Railroad study and 1937, the first year covered
by the series put out by the Dairen Chamber of Commerce. The number of
firms common to both years were noted and the ratio of paid-up capital
represented by the firms included in the sample type studies to total
estimated paid-up capital of relevant sectors compared.[20] Mining excluded,
estimated sectoral coverage of the sample type data is never less than
40% and with the exception of mining and metal and machinery at least
half the individual firms included in the 1937 statistics are also covered
by the earlier study. Thus, sectoral coverage is extensive enough to provide some basis for estimated global retained earnings and enough identical
firms are represented in both years to assure a measure of comparability
between the two series. Mining is so poorly represented in the earlier
study that it has been impossible to estimate global retained earnings in
the mining sector prior to 1937.

Unfortunately, this procedure throws no light on the representativeness
of the corporations included in these sample type studies. Estimates of
global retained earnings correspond to actual earnings retained only if
the rate of profit and the proportion of earnings retained by firms covered
in the surveys is typical of all firms. The corporate financial surveys
made by the Dairen Chamber of Commerce and the Industrial Bank over-lap
for the years 1939-1941. Comparisons between the rate of profits and the

---

[20]The estimates of industry-wide paid-up capital used are those presented
in Table 3.

proportion of earnings retained by firms by industry in the two studies show that the average rate of profits to paid-up capital and the proportion of earnings retained by firms included in the Dairen study were consistently above those of the Industrial Bank study for all industries except electricity and gas, transportation and communications where coverage was the same. For example, in metals and machinery the average ratios of profit to paid-up capital for firms included in the Dairen and Industrial Bank studies were respectively, 11.7% and 8.9% in 1939, 9.6% and 7.4% in 1940, and 5.7% and 4.8% in 1941. The average proportion of earnings retained was the same for both studies in 1939 while the Dairen rate was above that of the Industrial Bank for 1940 and 1941.

In view of the consistent upward difference of the ratios obtained on the basis of the Dairen study to those of the Industrial Bank, global estimates based on the Dairen study are greater than those based on the Industrial Bank study. Though the level of profit rates of the two studies is different in absolute terms, the trend of profit rates is one of decline between 1939 and 1941 in mining, metals and machinery, chemicals, ceramics, lumber and wood products.

Table 7 summarizes statistics gleaned from the three surveys of Manchoukuo corporate finances. Row A gives the amount of retained earnings by year and by industry as given in the sample studies, Row B indicates the number of companies included, Row C the amount of paid-up capital represented by firms included and Row D the estimated proportion of the paid-up capitalization of the sample firms to total capitalization of the particular sector.[21] In the earlier years, coverage is 25% or more except

---

[21] The industry-wide capitalization figures used in estimating sample study coverage are those presented in Table 3 except for those of transportation. See Table 4 for the figures used for capitalization in transportation.

TABLE 7

SAMPLE STUDY DATA ON RETAINED EARNINGS, NUMBER

		1930	1931	1932	1933	1934
GROUP A:						
Metal and	A[a]	210	407	299	974	2,316
Machinery	B	2	2	2	3	4
	C	26,000	26,000	26,000	61,500	85,000
	D					102%
Chemicals	A	-191	-177	212	794	481[b]
	B	12	12	13	13	13
	C	7,568	6,628	7,128	7,613	7,913
	D					25%
Lumber and	A	-16	-42[c]	82	350	345
Wood Pro-	B	7	5	6	7	7
ducts	C	1,890	1,580	1,830	1,890	2,155
	D					47%
Ceramics	A	141	-142	-871	829	868
	B	14	14	14	14	15
	C	5,984	5,984	5,384	5,284	5,825
						48%
GROUP B:						
Textiles	A	-510	-39	-126	-438	583
	B	6	5	6	6	7
	C	8,650	4,900	5,400	5,850	5,740
	D					44%
Foodstuffs	A	72	57	93	183	234
	B	5	5	5	6	11
	C	2,175	2,175	2,175	2,265	8,623
	D					40%
GROUP C						
Electri-	A	217	225	322	935	2,019
city & Gas	B	6	6	6	7	7
	C	33,638	33,638	33,638	33,925	34,113
	D					27%
MINING	A	6	-14	-6	66	41
	B	1	1	1	1	1
	C	375	375	375	375	600
	D					2%

1935	1937	1938	1939	1940	1941	1942
	12,050	13,331	14,472	16,569	12,475	7,039
	13	13	13	21	23	32
	128,700	203,050	266,850	427,850	649,450	743,500
	74%	81%	72%			
809	3,027	5,078	4,307	5,659	4,843	4,990
3	15	15	14	20	21	37
13,180	52,545	68,595	78,420	94,491	109,343	221,030
28%	49%	55%	11%			
92	789	1,591	2,604	4,312	4,717	3,063
2	5	6	6	10	9	7
850	3,675	4,775	5,550	18,025	18,200	17,500
14%	46%	51%	30%			
562	1,700	1,851	1,648	1,683	1,159	853
4	14	14	14	16	15	16
4,025	20,850	25,875	35,437	46,614	55,026	61,315
22%	94%	95%	85%			
447	1,522	4,218	4,392	7,400	7,358	7,854
2	6	7	7	13	12	18
5,625	23,922	29,172	33,421	52,025	55,500	96,580
34%	66%	58%	59%			
	444	2,143	3,640	5,346	4,319	4,581
	14	14	13	16	17	26
	20,325	21,625	29,025	44,475	47,505	72,835
	40%	42%	51%			
957	2,631	3,416	3,889	3,670	4,134	5,243
4	9	12	3	3	3	4
33,538	119,743	129,791	145,000	165,000	217,000	324,500
33%	85%	84%	92%	83%	77%	111%
47	1,175	2,239	842	-5,250	-10,243	-19,336
1	5	5	5	10	10	26
600	50,800	54,800	179,150	348,000	528,433	945,017
2%	66%	34%	47%	43%	48%	70%

TABLE 7 (cont'd)

		1937	1938	1939	1940	1941	1942
TRANSPORTATION	A	35,420	35,542	42,333	38,995	25,174	21,188
	B	8	8	6	8	9	16
	C	706,258	725,608	765,658	915,908	1,049,008	1,225,552
	D	97%	95%	85%	92%	95%	73%
COMMUNICATIONS	A	1,518	2,649	3,392	3,341	2,990	2,689
	B	1	1	1	1	1	1
	C	36,250	36,250	43,125	55,625	68,125	75,000
	D	100%	100%	100%	100%	100%	100%

a A: Retained earnings, unit: yen 1,000.
  B: Number of companies covered
  C: Paid-up capitalization of companies covered
  D: Estimated coverage of the surveys based on the ratio of paid-up capital of survey concerns to paid-up capital of the sector as cited in Table 3. In the case of transportation, the figures cited in Table 4, unadjusted for South Manchurian Railroad holdings of securities were used.

b The paid-up capitalization of company No. 1 included in the South Manchurian Railroad study of the chemical industry in 1934 has been excluded from the paid-up capital figure cited for the companies covered by the survey. This company was newly established and had not started to function by the end of 1934.

c The paid-up capital for company No. 7 covered by the South Manchurian Railroad survey of the lumber and wood industry has been excluded from item C for 1931 and 1932 as no data on dividends or earnings retained were available for those years.

SOURCES:

1930-1934/35: Minami Manshū Tetsudō (South Manchurian Railway Company), Manshū Kaisha Kōkahyō Shūsei, Kōgyōhen (Compilation of Records of Manchurian Corporations, Volume on Manufacturing), op. cit. For companies publishing data semi-annually, the figures relating to the date closest to the end of the calendar year were chosen. Where balance sheet data were made available at any time during the first three months of the calendar year, the figure was included in the series relating to the preceding year.

1937-1941: Dairen Shōkō Kaigisho (Dairen Chamber of Commerce), Manshū Jigyō Seiseki Bunseki (Analysis of Business Results of Manchurian Enterprises), op. cit.

1942: Manshu Kōgyō Ginkō (Industrial Bank of Manchou), Manshū Jigyō Kaisha Seiseki Bunseki (Analysis of Business Results of Manchurian Enterprises and Companies), op. cit.

for mining which as previously noted is poorly represented. After 1937,
coverage for chemicals, ceramics, metals and machinery, lumber and wood
products, electricity and gas, transportation, communications and mining
is at least 50% with a few exceptions.

The only way to estimate total retained earnings on a sector by sector
basis is to increase the figures on earnings retained by the sample firms
in proportion to the ratio of total sector paid-up capitslization to
sample sector paid-up capitalization. This procedure transmits the short-
comings present in data on aggregate paid-up capitalization of incorporated
businesses to the estimates of earnings retained by these firms. This
method assumes that the paid-up capital of a group of firms is the best
measure of their share of earnings retained by a particular industry. But
the relationship between a firm's paid-up capital and earnings retained
depends on the role of other types of financing, the level of profits and
the proportion of profits retained among other factors. If these relation-
ships with respect to the firms included in the sample study differ from
those of the whole industry, industry-wide estimates of retained earnings
will be correspondingly inaccurate.

In Table 8, industry-wide retained earnings are estimated for metals
and machinery, chemicals, ceramics, lumber and wood products, textiles,
foodstuffs, electricity and gas, mining, transportation and communications
for the years from 1930 through 1942. No estimates were made for mining
prior to 1937 due to inadequate coverage. Except for transportation and
communications during the earlier years, estimates for 1930-1935 and
1937-1942 are based on the ratio of paid-up capital of corporations
covered by the sample studies to total paid-up capital in the particular
sector. In estimating retained earnings for 1940-1942, retained earnings

TABLE 8

ESTIMATED INDUSTRY-WIDE RETAINED EARNINGS IN MANCHOUKUO, 1930-1942   (unit: yen 1,000)

Industry	1930	1931	1932	1933	1934	1935	1936	1937	1938	1939	1940	1941	1942
Metal and Machinery	420	798	610	1,149	2,316	7,029	7,924	16,268	16,397	20,116			
Chemicals	-493	-515	598	2,850	1,934	2,872	4,265	6,175	9,242	39,151	52,213	36,183	22,801
Lumber & Wood	-23	-71	124	696	731	655	1,319	1,712	3,118	8,671			
Ceramics	168	-173	-1,237	1,635	1,805	2,507	2,352	1,202	1,944	1,945			
Textiles	-556	-74	-227	-986	1,318	1,292	1,713	2,313	7,255	7,422	42,444	41,687	34,569
Foodstuffs	446	348	592	1,523	583	761	1,022	1,110	5,100	7,134			
Electricity & Gas	513	525	782	3,067	7,470	2,900	2,584	3,105	4,065	4,239	4,441	5,374	5,243
Mining	---	---	---	---	---	---	---	1,786	6,583	1,793	-12,233	-21,305	-27,650
Transportation	-1,265	-1,945	37,017	13,293	13,197	13,474	11,143	36,483	37,319	49,953	42,895	26,433	29,028
Communications	---	---	---	252	1,227	1,628	1,379	1,518	2,649	3,932	3,341	2,990	2,689
TOTAL	-790	-1,107	38,259	23,479	30,581	33,118	33,701	72,272	93,672	144,356	133,101	91,362	66,680

See pages 60-64, Table 9 and Table 10 for an explanation of the procedures used in estimating industry-wide retained earnings.

included in the sample studies have been combined to correspond to the
A, B, and C groups of industries.

The sample studies yielded no data on retained earnings in 1936 or in
1935 for metal and machinery, and foodstuffs. The sample study ratios of
retained earnings to paid-up capital were computed for 1933-1935 and 1937-
1938. The ratio for each industry moved erratically from year to year
with the exception of that for electricity and gas. Nevertheless, the
average of the ratio in 1937 and that of the last year for which it was
available in the earlier years was taken to represent the ratio of retained
earnings to paid-up capital operative in 1936 and 1935 in the case of metals,
machinery and foodstuffs. This ratio was then applied to the paid-up
capital figures cited in Table 3, and the resulting figure used as the
estimated earnings retained. The ratios and paid-up capital figures used
in this crude process are reproduced in Table 9.

The South Manchurian Railroad study of corporate finances covering the
years prior to 1936 did not deal with transportation and communications.
This omission can be remedied in part by examining the finances of the most
important company in each sector, the South Manchurian Railroad and the
Manchuria Telegraph and Telephone Company.[22] The latter company was organized in 1933 to monopolize communications in Manchoukuo. As of 1935,
the paid-up capital of the South Manchurian Railroad amounted to yen 512
million[23] which accounted for 80% of paid-up capital in the transportation

---

[22]The Japanese name for the company is Manshū Denshin Denwa K.K.

[23]South Manchurian Railroad, Fifth Report on Progress in Manchuria, op.
cit., p. 139. The yen 512 million figure cited in the text was obtained
by adjusting the amount of capital stock subscribed for that not yet called.

TABLE 9

FACTORS USED IN ESTIMATING RETAINED EARNINGS FOR 1935 AND 1936

(unit: yen 1,000)

Industry	Estimated Ratio of Retained Earnings to Paid-up Capital[a]	1935		1936	
		Paid-up Capital[b]	Estimated Earnings Retained[c]	Paid-up Capital[b]	Estimated Earnings Retained[c]
Metal & Machinery	6.05	116,186	7,029	130,970	7,924
Chemicals	5.95			71,685	4,265
Ceramics	11.1			21,190	2,352
Lumber & Wood	16.1			8,190	1,319
Textiles	7.1			24,138	1,713
Foodstuffs	2.4	31,713	761	42,572	1,022
Electricity & Gas	2.5			103,345	2,584

[a] The ratio of retained earnings to paid-up capital in 1937 averaged with that of the last year covered by the South Manchurian Railroad study of corporate finances.

[b] The figures on paid-up capital are those presented in Table 3.

[c] Earnings retained were estimated by multiplying the amount of paid-up capital for a given industry by the averaged ratio of retained earnings to paid-up capital.

sector.[24] Thus by including the earnings retained by these two companies
in the statistics compiled, all of the communications industry would be
accounted for after 1933 and the bulk of transportation prior to 1937.

Financial statements are available which give data on the profits and
dividends paid by these companies. Since profits less dividends disbursed
approximate earnings retained, the time series of earnings retained in
transportation and communications can be extended back into time. No
attempt was made to estimate industry-wide retained earnings in transportation for the years before 1937 because the South Manchurian Railroad
accounted for 80% of paid-up capital in transportation in 1935 and the crude
methods of estimation employed in this study could not have improved noticeably on this figure. The retained earnings estimates based on the financial
data of the South Manchurian Railroad and the Manchuria Telegraph and Telephone Company are presented in Table 10.

Returning to the estimates of retained earnings presented in Table
8, 1930 and 1931 were years of net dissaving for the industries covered,
aggregated retained earnings being minus yen 790,000 and minus yen 1,107,000.
During 1933-1942, earnings retained made a positive contribution to funds
available for investment. In 1932, estimated earnings retained reached
yen 38 million but the South Manchurian Railroad provided virtually all
of this amount. Between 1933 and 1936 earnings retained fluctuated between yen 23.5 million and yen 33.7 million each year. In 1937 the amount
of earnings retained starts to rise sharply and continues to do so
through 1939 when a peak of yen 144.4 million was reached. In 1940,

---

[24]Total paid-up capital in the transportation sector amounted to
yen 639 million prior to any adjustment for securities held by the South
Manchurian Railroad in other companies.

TABLE 10

ESTIMATED EARNINGS RETAINED BY THE SOUTH MANCHURIAN RAILROAD AND

THE MANCHURIA TELEGRAPH AND TELEPHONE COMPANY PRIOR TO 1937

(unit: yen 1,000)

South Manchurian Railroad

	I Profits	II Dividends	III: I minus II Estimated Retained Earnings
1930	21,673	22,938	- 1,265
1931	12,598	14,543	- 1,945
1932	61,288	24,271	37,017
1933	42,921	29,628	13,293
1934	46,467	33,270	13,197
1935	49,624	36,150	13,474
1936	50,173	39,030	11,143

Manchuria Telegraph and Telephone Company

1933 (Sept-Dec)	839.5	587.5	252
1934	2,989.5	1,762.5	1,227
1935	3,390.5	1,762.5	1,628
1936	3,553.5	2,175.0	1,378.5

Sources: Ōkurashō (Japanese Ministry of Finance) Nihonjin Kaigai
Katsudō ni Kan suru Rekishiteki Chōsa (A Historical Inves-
tigation of the Overseas Activity of Japanese), op. cit.
South Manchurian Railroad data: Appendices 10, 12.
Manchuria Telegraph and Telephone data: p. 623.

the figure declines slightly to yen 133.1 million and then falls off
sharply to yen 91.4 million in 1941 and yen 66.7 million in 1942. This
decline in the absolute contribution of earnings retained to funds
available for investment came at a time when the sectors covered were
undergoing a terrific expansion. Thus, the relative contribution of
retained earnings fell off sharply.

Earnings retained declined for the simple reason that profits were
falling in all Manchurian industries. The ratio of profits to shareholders' equity, defined as the book value of paid-up-capital plus reserves
and the carry-over from the previous period, in nine Manchurian industries
is graphed in Figure 5. The downturn in the profit ratio occurred at the
end of 1938 or 1939, and except for transportation fell steadily thereafter.
Profits fell because modern industries were caught in a price/cost squeeze.
For example, the distribution of iron and steel was rigidly controlled
through the Japan Manchousuo Trading Company and price controls were
effective. But the economic authorities were less successful in controlling the prices of raw materials and labor costs. The dividend rates
paid by these industries declined somewhat but not enough to keep the
ratio of earnings retained at previous levels. The decline in the
absolute amount of earnings retained by these industries was the natural
consequence of the decline in profits coupled with the lower proportion
of earnings retained.

Thusfar there has been no mention of depreciation allowances, which
can be another form of internal financing. In advanced countries, depreciation allowances which are counted as an expense of business operations
are an important source of funds for investment. Theoretically, the
level of depreciation allowances should depend on the value and life span
of the fixed assets of a corporation but in practice they depend more

FIGURE 5

THE RATIO OF PROFITS TO

SHAREHOLDERS' EQUITY IN MANCHURIAN INDUSTRIES, 1937-1942

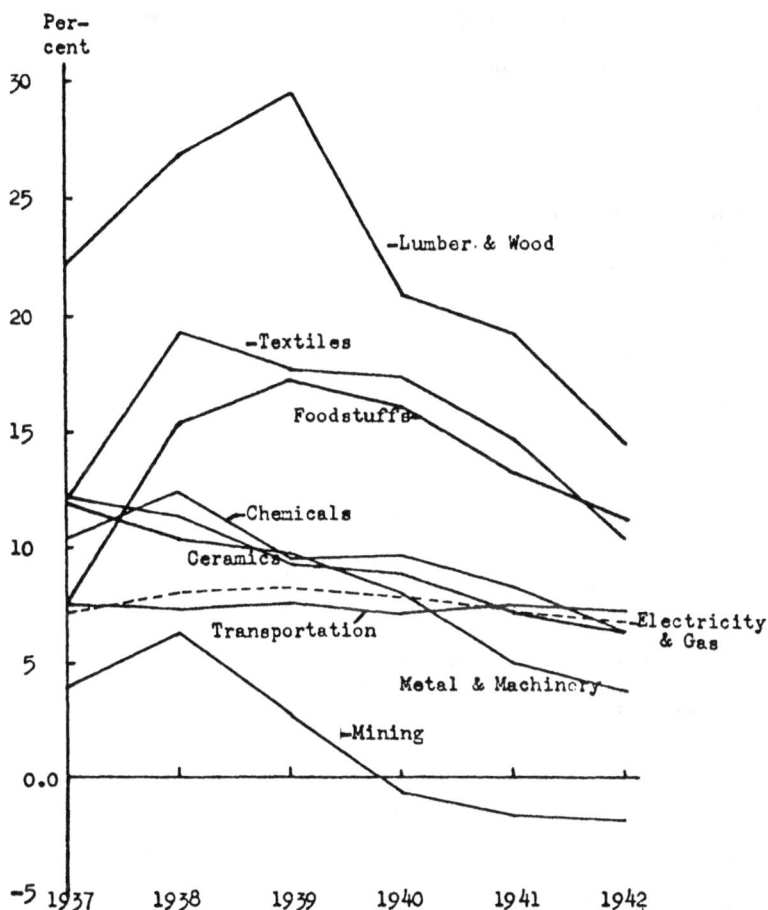

Sources:
1937-1941: Dairen Shōkō Kaigisho(Dairen Chamber of Commerce),
op. cit., 1937-1941.
1942: Manshū Kōgyō Ginkō(Industrial Bank of Manchou),
Manshū Jigyō Kaisha Seiseki Bunseki(Analysis of
Business Results of Manchurian Enterprises and
Companies), 1942.

on the tax laws. In countries with high taxes on business, the tax laws limit the amount which can be charged to depreciation and written off as a business expense. However, in Manchuria business taxes were only 7% so they were not an important consideration.[25]

The balance sheet studies for 1937-1942 provide data on the annual depreciation allowances of the companies included. The studies list the amount of depreciation and the ratio of depreciation to total fixed assets for each company and each industry as a whole. This information is presented in Table 11. No attempt has been made to estimate industry-wide depreciation because after allowing for replacement it is doubtful that depreciation allowances made any contribution to investment. Furthermore no data is available on depreciation prior to 1937.

During 1937 and 1938, the rates of depreciation in the chemical, metal and machinery, mining and electricity industries were as high as 7.6% and always at least 3.1%. However, during 1939 and 1940 when investment reached a peak, the rate of depreciation failed to keep pace with the growth in fixed assets. In metals and machinery, the most important industry in the five year plans, the rate of depreciation was only 0.4% and 0.9% in these years. The rate of depreciation in the transportation industry was steady during the period, ranging from 3.1% to 2.5%. This stability was due to the South Manchurian Railroad which was always concerned with its financial soundness. The depreciation allowance of the Railroad accounted for about two-thirds of all depreciation included in the studies on business results.

---

[25] The Manchoukuo Yearbook 1942, op. cit., p. 218. This tax rate was levied after January 1941 on net business income exceeding yen 1,000 a year.

TABLE 11

DATA ON DEPRECIATION AND THE RATE OF DEPRECIATION

IN SELECTED MANCHURIAN INDUSTRIES, 1937-1941

(unit: yen 1,000)

Industry	1937	1938	1939	1940	1941
Chemicals	3,411[a]	4,014	2,017	2,088	4,501
	6.6%[b]	7.6%	3.0%	2.4%	4.6%
Metals &	556	748	1,064	3,546	14,982
Machinery	6.6%	5.7%	0.4%	0.9%	2.7%
Lumber & Wood	434	205	195	38	395
	10.3%	4.4%	4.3%	0.5%	4.1%
Ceramics	1,228	1,719	1,581	953	1,286
	6.9%	7.6%	5.1%	2.2%	3.1%
Textiles	1,800	2,980	4,189	3,674	3,530
	8.8%	10.7%	13.5%	7.6%	7.0%
Foodstuffs	426	933	1,389	1,777	1,400
	3.2%	4.1%	4.7%	3.7%	2.3%
Mining	1,392	151	195	387	2,520
	4.1%	6.3%	1.0%	0.1%	0.6%
Electricity	760	455	390	790	990
& Gas	7.6%	3.1%	0.2%	0.3%	0.3%
Transportation	22,238	32,449	33,555	26,740	42,632
	2.5%	3.4%	3.3%	2.4%	3.6%
Communications	2,131	2,993	4,060	3,293	4,028
	3.1%	3.8%	4.1%	2.6%	2.5%

[a]The amount of annual depreciation of companies included in the Dairen Chamber of Commerce volumes on business results.

[b]The ratio of annual depreciation to total fixed assets less work in progress.

Source: Dairen Shōkō Kaigisho (Dairen Chamber of Commerce), Manshū Jigyō Seiseki Bunseki (Analysis of Business Results of Manchurian Enterprises), op. cit.

Section 3.   Financing Manchoukuo Industrial Development

through the Extension of Loans

Statistics are available on loans extended by Manchurian financial
institutions from 1932 through 1945 classified by the type of lending
institution.   The financial institutions covered are: domestic ordinary
banks; Japanese banks; Chinese banks; European banks; The Central Bank of
Manchou; and the Industrial Bank of Manchou.[26]

Data on the uses to which the loans of these institutions were put
are available from 1938.   The recipients of the credit extended are classified as follows: commerce; manufacturing; construction; agriculture;
mining; soya beans and bean products; and others.   Only the loans extended
to manufacturing and mining are included in this study.   Loans by Manchurian
financial institutions to manufacturing and mining were estimated for the
years 1932 through 1937.   The proportion of mining and maufacturing loans
to total loans made by each type of financial institution was calculated
for 1938 and 1939, the first two years for which such data are available.
These two figures were averaged and the resulting ratio was taken as the
estimated percentage which loans to mining and manufacturing formed of
total loans during the years prior to 1938.   This estimated percentage was
then applied to total loans made by type of Manchurian financial institution.

---

[26]After 1937, extra-territoriality was abolished and all banking
institutions fell uniformly under the control of the Manchoukuo Government.
However, the distinction between Japanese, Chinese, European and domestic
ordinary banks was continued in the financial statistics.   The distinction
maintained was to some extent a historical one.   All of these institutions
were basically commercial banks.   The Central Bank of Manchou and the
Industrial Bank of Manchou were special institutions erected by the Government to carry out specific functions and fall into a completely different
category.

It is impossible to gauge how typical the averaged 1938/1939 relative share of loans to mining and manufacturing is of the earlier years. The share of loans made by all Manchurian financial institutions to mining and manufacturing rose from 15% to 25% between 1938 and 1939 due to the heightened tempo of industrialization. But the increased volume of loans made by the Industrial Bank was responsible for most of this rise. The proportion of loans made to manufacturing and mining by financial organs other than the Industrial Bank was the same in 1938 and 1939 and changed little through 1941.[27] In view of this stability, it is assumed here that this share was similar during the early years although the assumption has none too firm a foundation.

The Central Bank of Manchou's main function was that of a central bank but it was permitted to operate as an ordinary commercial bank. The Central Bank could have been active in extending loans to mining and manufacturing before the establishment of the Industrial Bank. However, except for some few loans extended to one of the oil companies for drilling and the Manchuria Electric Company, the Central Bank was never important as a direct supplier of credit for mining and manufacturing although it was important in rediscounting commercial paper, particularly that relating

---

[27]The percentage share of loans to mining and manufacturing made by the following institutions was:

	1938	1939
Domestic Ordinary Banks	11%	10%
Japanese Banks	3.8%	3.6%
Chinese Banks	6.1%	7.8%
European Banks	3.9%	0.0%
Central Bank	NA	2.7% (1940: 3.7%)
Industrial Bank	29%	50%

Source: Minami Manshū Tetsudō (South Manchurian Railway Company), Tōkei Kihō ... (Quarterly of Statistics...), op. cit., No. 1 (Nov., 1941), pp. 120-121.

to the activities of Mangyō.

The statistics on loans by use combine a number of categories such as: loans backed by securities or commercial paper; loans financed by rediscount operations; and overdrafts. Consequently, no distinction has been made in the statistics on loans by use regarding the time limit of the lending activity. Theoretically, short term loans are used to augment working capital while longer term credit is for the expansion of plant. In practice, the distinction between short and long term loans breaks down. If short term loans are renewed regularly, they become long term loans. After World War II in Japan, the automatic renewal of short term loans was standard practice so inability to distinguish between loans made for the purpose of extending plant and equipment and those made to provide working capital is not a serious defect.

Loans to the mining and manufacturing industries in Manchoukuo came not only from banks. Interfirm loans were also important. The South Manchurian Railroad and Mangyō were both large creditors. Loans made by the South Manchurian Railroad have been excluded from Table 12 on total loans outstanding because every attempt has been made to include all resources available to the Railroad for investment in any form. Since loans extended by the Company were provided from the pool of financial resources collected through the sale of stock, bonds and the retention of earnings, the inclusion of loans made by the Railroad would constitute duplication. In line with the liabilities approach to the investment resources of the South Manchurian Railroad, loans made to the Company have been included.[28]

---

[28]In compiling series on investment in Manchurian industry, the author has been mainly concerned with providing the greatest possible coverage and avoiding double counting. As stated earlier, the claims approach has been

TABLE 12

THE FINANCING OF MANCHOUKUO MANUFACTURING, MINING, TRANSPORTATION AND COMMUNICATIONS

THROUGH THE EXTENSION OF LOANS, 1932-1945.   (unit: yen 1,000)

Item	1932	1933	1934	1935	1936	1937	1938	1939	1940	1941	1942	1943	1944
Manufacturing[a]													
Private Banks	13,162	11,149	18,383	16,597	20,023	14,410	23,291	29,425	66,293	110,013	191,613	826,894	1,790,451
Central Bank	3,966	3,325	5,284	5,472	6,315	6,791	13,439	23,521	32,347	30,301	27,778	}	}
Industrial Bank						38,954	92,059	306,030	623,649	338,267	389,293	}	}
Mining													
Private Banks	744	623	991	1,026	1,184	1,273	43	56	657	927	929	145,396	382,395
Central Bank							2,520	5,404	5,107	8,449	1,272	}	}
Industrial Bank						5,656	17,806	72,139	125,334	89,604	32,452	}	}
Loans by Mangyō in Manchoukuo							3,000	66,000	170,000	471,000	495,000	629,000	695,000
Total Loans Outstanding	17,872	15,097	24,658	23,095	27,522	67,084	152,158	502,575	1,023,327	1,048,561	1,138,337	1,601,290	2,867,846
Annual Increase in Loans Outstanding		-2,775	9,561	-1,563	4,427	99,562	85,074	350,417	520,752	25,234	89,776	462,953	1,266,556
Net Japanese Loans to[b] Four Sectors, Mangyō Excluded			12,000	140,000	-16,250	158,050	11,200	94,000					
TOTAL ANNUAL NET LOANS		-2,775	21,561	138,437	-11,823	197,612	96,274	444,417	520,752	25,234	89,776	462,953	1,266,556

[a] The figures on loans made to manufacturing and mining by private banks and the Central Bank of Manchou were estimated to have been in the same proportion to the total amount of loans outstanding as in 1938/1939.

[b] Data from 1940 onward have been excluded as only gross figures are available for these years.

TABLE 12 (continued)

SOURCES

1. Loans made by private banks and the Central Bank:

   1932-1937: (Total Loans) Manshū Chūō Ginkō (Central Bank of Manchou), Manshū Chūō Ginkō Jūnenshi(Ten Year History of the Central Bank of Manchou), Hsinking, 1942, Appendix 10.

   1938-1942: Minami Manshū Tetsudō (South Manchurian Railway Company), Tōkei Kihō ... (Quarterly of Statistics ...), op. cit., No. 1 (Nov. 1941), No. 2 (March 1942), No. 3 (1943).

   1943-1944: Northeast China Economic Commission, XIX, op. cit., Appendix 16A. The loans of all banks by use are combined for these years.

2. Loans made by the Industrial Bank:

   1937-1941: Kōgyō Ginkō (Industrial Bank), Manshū Kōgyō Ginkō Setsu (Industrial Bank of Manchou Report), Hsinking, April 1942, p. 21.

   1942: Minami Manshū Tetsudō (South Manchurian Railway Company), Tōkei Kihō ... (Quarterly of Statistics ...), op. cit., No. 3 (1943).

   1943-1944: As in 1.

3. Loans made by Mangyō in Manchoukuo:
   "Heavy Industry in Manchoukuo" op. cit., p. 71.

4. Japanese Loans:
   1932-1940: The Manchoukuo Yearbook 1942, op. cit., pp. 290-291.

As explained previously, the assets approach has been followed in the case of Mangyō. Stocks and bonds held by Mangyō have been omitted because they have been counted elsewhere as liabilities of the issuing firms. Loans made by Mangyō must be included as they have not been included in other series. Loans to affiliates were an important form of Mangyō investment. At the end of 1942, Mangyō investments in Manchoukuo amounted to yen 1,781 million of which yen 495 million or 36% took the form of loans.[29]

All the loans made by Mangyō in Manchoukuo have been included in the series. Mangyō and the Industrial Bank of Manchou maintained a close relationship. The Industrial Bank is known to have had large holdings of Mangyō bonds and it undoubtedly made loans to Mangyō. One should exclude loans made by the Industrial Bank to Mangyō from either the series on loans made by Mangyō to other firms or from the series on Industrial Bank loans to Mangyō in order to avoid double counting, but data on Industrial Bank loans include no information on recipient firms.

Statistics on Japanese investment in Manchoukuo show that net Japanese loans to Mangyō were low, yen 10 million in 1937, yen 38.5 million in 1938, yen 20 million in 1939 and minus yen 28 million in 1940.[30] Yet during these years, loans to Mangyō rose steadily:

---

followed in compiling the series presented in this chapter. However, once interfirm investment takes place, the claims approach will result in double counting as the claims of the investors in the company holding interfirm investments are counted as well as the claims of the company holding securities in another firm. In the case of the South Manchurian Railroad, the conventional claims approach in which attention is directed to the liabilities side of the balance sheet has been followed. Thus, loans made to the South Manchurian Railroad have been included while those made by the Railroad to other firms have been excluded.

[29]"Heavy Industry in Manchoukuo," op. cit., p. 71.

[30]The Manchoukuo Yearbook, 1942, op. cit., pp. 290-291.

Loans Outstanding to Mangyō, 1938-1941[31]

November 1938	117 million yen
November 1939	369 million yen
November 1940	664 million yen
May 1941	763 million yen

This increase in Mangyō's debt must either have been met through intra-Mangyō transfers which do not appear in the statistics on Japanese investments in Manchoukuo, or through loans from organizations within Manchoukuo.[32] The Industrial Bank of Manchou was the logical supplier of credit loans to Mangyō. Yet during the same years total Industrial Bank loans to mining and industry at the end of the year amounted to:[33]

1938	110 million yen
1939	378 million yen
1940	749 million yen
1941	428 million yen

The debt of Mangyō in November of 1938 and May of 1941 is greater than the total volume of Industrial Bank loans to mining and industry at the end of these two years. The Industrial Bank surely supplied credit to

---

[31]Ibid., p. 296.

[32]Mangyō controlled concerns operating in Japan as well as Manchoukuo until the end of 1941 when the company was reorganized and Mangyō's Japanese subsidiaries disposed of. The financial relations between Mangyō subsidiaries located in Manchoukuo and those located in Japan were complex and certainly intimate. The author feels that transfers from Mangyō subsidiaries in Japan to those in Manchoukuo could easily have taken place without being reflected in the statistics on Japanese investment in Manchoukuo.

[33]See Table 12 on loans. Loans made by the Industrial Bank to Mangyō may not be included in the classification of loans made to mining and manufacturing which appears in the financial statistics. In the statistics on corporate finances Mangyō appears in the category "holding companies" or "financial companies" rather than under mining and manufacturing. However, the author feels that loans to Mangyō were included in the mining and manufacturing category of Industrial Bank loan data as there is no other appropriate category.

firms other than Mangyō so it is clear that Mangyō had sources of credit
other than the Industrial Bank. Whatever portion Industrial Bank loans
formed of Mangyō resources for investment, constitutes double counting
and an upward bias in the statistics on loans.[34]

Total outstanding loans to mining, manufacturing and transportation
were negligible until 1937 when the figure stood at yen 100 million.
With the inauguration of the five year plan, the establishment of the
Industrial Bank and Mangyō, loans outstanding to mining and manufacturing
became an important factor in financing the expansion of these sectors.
Total loans outstanding, roughly doubled each year between 1938 and 1940
when they amounted to yen 1,074 million. In 1941, they levelled off to
yen 1,088 million and rose only slightly to yen 1,144 million in 1942.
Loans extended by Mangyō and the Industrial Bank accounted for a large
portion of the total in the years following 1937. In 1938, when these
institutions had been functioning little more than one year they accounted
for 62% of total loans outstanding in mining, manufacturing and transportation and at the end of 1942 their share had risen to 80%.

Section 4:   Total Investment by Component Type Supplied Annually to
             Manchoukuo Manufacturing, Mining, Transportation and
             Communications, 1931-1942.

Table 13 presents a composite picture of annual increments in capital

---

[34]In 1939, Mangyō obtained yen 380 million in new capital. Of this
amount, yen 200 million was loaned by the Industrial Bank. (Far Eastern
Survey, Vol. IX (March 3, 1940), p. 73.) Thus, if this figure is correct, at the end of 1939, 53% of Industrial Bank loans to mining and
manufacturing had been extended to Mangyō. This is the only information
that has been found on Industrial Bank loans to Mangyō. It was deemed
best not to adjust the loan statistics for a single year as this would
seriously cloud the estimated increase in loans outstanding to mining
and manufacturing in the following year.

TABLE 13

CAPITAL BY COMPONENT TYPE SUPPLIED ANNUALLY TO MANCHOUKUO MANUFACTURING,

MINING, TRANSPORTATION AND COMMUNICATIONS, 1931-1942.

(unit: yen 1,000)

	Annual Increase In			Earnings		
	Paid-up Capital	Bonds	Loans	Retained	TOTAL	Index
1931	-1,682	19,475	NA	-1,107	16,686	
1932	22,966	73,475	NA	38,259	134,700	100
1933	168,560	-4,977	-2,775	23,479	184,287	137
1934	97,500	186,225	21,561	30,581	335,867	249
1935	84,431	110,375	138,437	33,113	366,361	272
1936	111,778	188,275	-11,823	33,701	321,931	239
1937	355,688	27,975	197,612	72,272	653,547	485
1938	288,768	139,587	96,274	93,672	618,301	459
1939	1,005,629	183,325	444,417	144,356	1,777,727	1320
1940	599,546	501,493	520,752	133,101	1,754,892	1303
1941	713,133	385,380	25,234	91,362	1,215,109	902
1942	1,110,045	374,930	89,776	66,680	1,641,431	1219
1943			462,953			
1944			1,266,556			

All data are in current prices

Sources: Paid-up Capital and Bonds: See Table 3.
          Loans: Table 12.
          Retained Earnings: Table 8.

available to all four sectors being studied while the distinction between the component types of capital has been maintained. The annual increments available through increases in stocks, bonds and loans outstanding have been obtained by subtracting the total for a given year from the total for the previous year. Retained earnings which are a net addition in any year were included as estimated in Section 2 of this chapter.

Total annual investment has been graphed in Figure 6. The sharp rise during 1939 and the decline in 1941 are the most striking aspects of the contours graphed. Upon studying the individual components as graphed in Figure 7, it is clear that the increase in 1939 was a general one reflected in all four components. Increases in paid-up capital provided yen 1,006 million or 57% of capital made available to the four sectors that year. This figure represented a three-fold increase over that for any previous year. Increases in loans outstanding provided yen 444 million or 25% of total capital available in 1939. This figure was more than double any previous annual increment in loans and loans made by the Industrial Bank were responsible for yen 268 million or 60%. Retained earning reached a peak of yen 144 million and accounted for 10% of total capital supplied to the four sectors in 1939.

In 1940, roughly the same level of investment was maintained though the component composition differred markedly. Retained earnings fell slightly from the 1939 level and the other three components each contributed between yen 500 and yen 600 million. The increase in paid-up capital during the year was only 60% of that in 1939 and the absolute decrease in the contribution of paid-up capital was compensated for by a rise in that of bonds and loans.

FIGURE 6

TOTAL ANNUAL INCREASE IN CAPITAL AVAILABLE TO MANCHURIAN

MINING, MANUFACTURING, TRANSPORTATION AND COMMUNICATIONS, 1931-1942

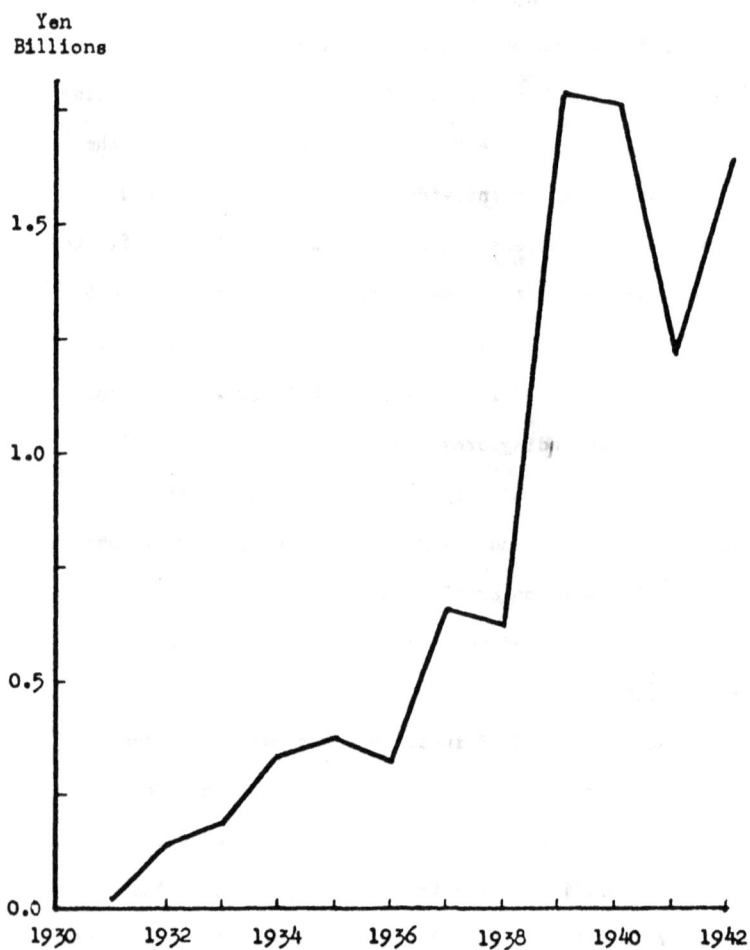

All data are in current prices.
Sources: As in Table 13

FIGURE 7

CAPITAL COMPONENTS AVAILABLE TO MANCHURIAN MINING,

MANUFACTURING, TRANSPORTATION AND COMMUNICATIONS, 1931-1942

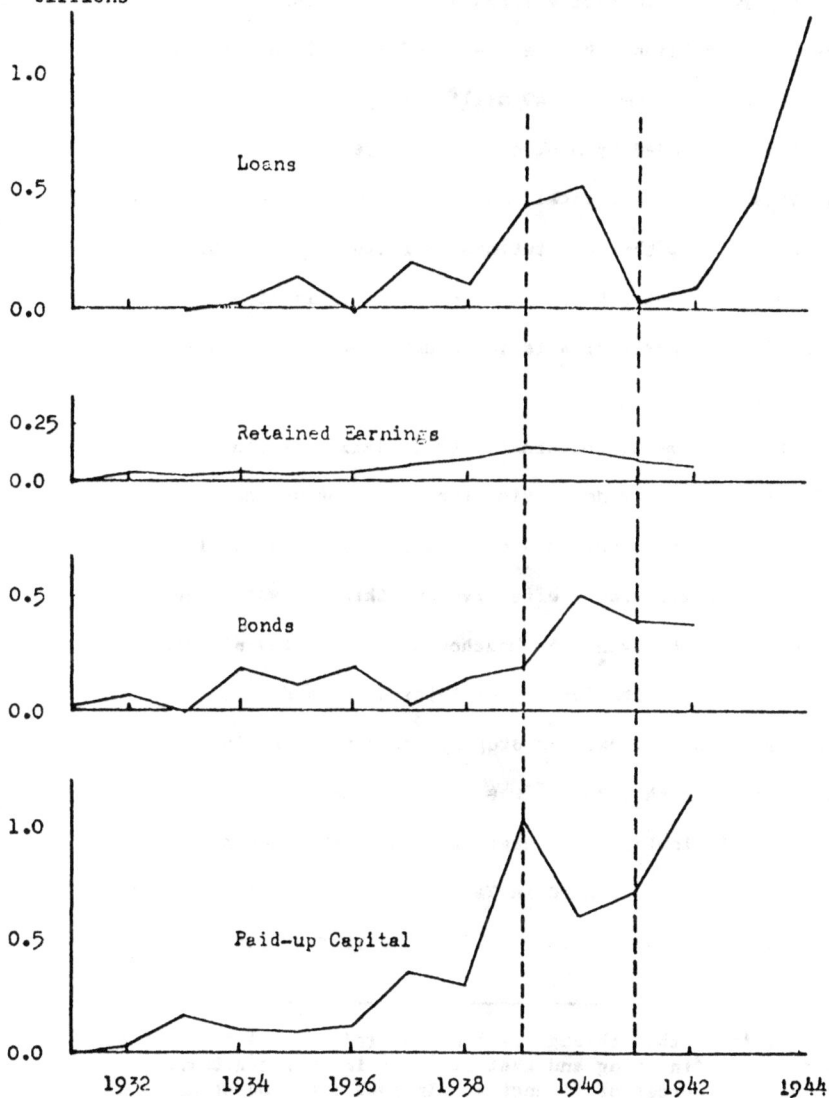

All data are in current prices.

Source: Table 13

The drop in the amount of new capital made available to manufacturing, mining, transportation and communications in 1941 was due to a
reduction in the contribution from loans. During 1940, the amount of
loans outstanding rose by yen 521 million and in 1941 the figure was an
insignificant yen 25 million. Between 1940 and 1941, loans extended by
the Industrial Bank fell from yen 749 million to yen 428 million. At
the same time loans extended by Mangyō rose from yen 170 million to yen
471 million. Thus, though the total amount of loans outstanding between
1940 and 1941 was stable, the institutional structure of lending changed
considerably. Unfortunately, information on the details of Mangyō and
Industrial Bank lending activities is inadequate for a clear interpreta-
tion of this shift.[35]

In 1941, the Government, concerned with inflationary tendencies attempted to slow investment by decreasing the amount of new capital. A
credit policy which either stabilized or reduced the amount of loans
outstanding would be particularly effective and this is exactly what
happened. However, in the event the Manchoukuo authorities directed the
Industrial Bank to curtail its lending activities it is difficult to
understand why Mangyō was allowed to step up its lending activity so
sharply. It is possible that Mangyō was permitted to extend more credit
to its subsidiaries following the reorganization of the company in 1941.

In Table 14 the data presented in Table 13 have been combined for
1931-1936, the pre-plan years, and 1937-1941, the years of the first five

---

[35]The author feels that through 1941 Mangyō relied on its Japanese
subsidiaries for loan financing and that starting in 1942 the Company
turned to Manchoukuo sources of financing. In 1942 loans outstanding to
Mangyō fell by yen 517 million probably due to the repayment of interfirm loans made by Japanese subsidiaries following the 1941 reorganization
of the company.

year plan, the series for 1942 are listed separately and then all items
totalled. During the period as a whole, corporate shares accounted for
51% of additions to investment funds, bonds for 24%, loans for 17% and
retained earnings for 8%. If one compares the pre-plan and plan periods,
some striking shifts are evident. Paid-up capital and loans become more
important as sources of capital while bonds and retained earnings become
less so.

TABLE 14

RECAPITULATION OF TABLE 13: CAPITAL BY COMPONENT TYPE SUPPLIED
ANNUALLY TO MANCHOUKUO MANUFACTURING, MINING, TRANSPORTATION
AND COMMUNICATIONS, 1931-1936, 1937-1941, AND 1942

(unit: yen 1,000)

| | Increase In | | | | |
	Paid-up Capital	Bonds	Loans	Earnings Retained	TOTAL
1931-1936	483,553 36%	572,848 42%	145,400 10.5%	158,031 11.5%	1,359,832 100%
1937-1941	2,962,764 49%	1,237,760 21%	1,284,289 21%	534,763 9%	6,019,576 100%
1942	1,110,045 68%	374,930 23%	89,776 5%	66,680 4%	1,641,431 100%
TOTAL	4,556,362 51%	2,185,538 24%	1,519,465 17%	759,474 8%	9,020,839 100%

Sources: As in Table 13.

In the pre-plan period, additions to paid-up capital provided
36% of total additions while during the years from 1937-1941 the figure
was 49%. The mining sector increased greatly during the plan period and
most of the increase was financed by a rise in the amount of paid-up
capital. Furthermore, as mentioned earlier, the existence of Mangyō
assured a ready market for shares issued in the manufacturing and mining

sector. Mangyō, as a holding company, was more interested in the purchase of company shares than bonds since a voice in the control of the companies was assured to a large shareholder.

Transportation and communications were the only sectors where bond financing was on a par with the issuance of shares as a means of corporate financing. Manchurian transportation and communications grew proportionately less than the mining and manufacturing sectors because the former sectors were initially far more developed and this explains the decline in the share of bond financing after 1937. Thus, these shifts in the relative importance of different investment components are more readily explained by institutional factors rather than economic factors during the Manchoukuo Period.

CHAPTER III

THE INSTITUTIONS SUPPLYING THE

CAPITAL FOR MANCHURIAN ECONOMIC DEVELOPMENT

Analyzing the sources of investment in Manchurian mining, manufacturing, transportation and communications is as important a task as compiling data on total investment in these sectors. In the Manchurian case, the level of total investment depended greatly on the flow of funds from Japan to the South Manchurian Railroad and Mangyō. Had either the Railroad or Mangyō failed to exist, Japan's contribution would have been less and total investment would have decreased correspondingly. Without these institutions, the sectors under study would have absorbed investment at a much lower rate.

Estimating the amount of capital supplied by groups or organizations fostering Manchurian economic development is difficult because the interrelations of the relevant groups were complex. Some of these complexities were touched upon in the previous chapter on the amount of capital available annually to Manchoukuo corporations, the final users of the investment funds. Ideally, the groups supplying investment funds for Manchurian industrial development should be divided into foreign and domestic sources of capital. Each of these categories should then be subdivided into Government, special organizations such as the South Manchurian Railroad and Mangyo and the general public but as usual the statistical series seldom conform to the data requirements of the theorist.

Data are available on investments made by the South Manchurian Railroad and Mangyō. Both of these institutions contained domestic, foreign,
private and government investment but their disaggregation is frequently
impossible. The contribution made by the domestic private sector can
only be estimated as a residual. Yet it is important to estimate the
contribution or lack of contribution made by the domestic private sector.
Whenever the private sector is as important as it was in agrarian Manchoukuo
and it fails to participate in developing the modern sector of the economy,
the schism between the modern and traditional sectors will prevail. Until
the gap between the modern and traditional sectors is bridged, a colonial
economic pattern will prevail in which a modern economic island will be
developed apart from the surrounding native economy. This was, in effect,
the situation in Manchoukuo.

Section 1: The Routing of Investment Funds to Manchoukuo Industry

An understanding of the routes followed by investment funds between
the supplier and the ultimate user is essential to the compilation of time
series on the volume of capital provided by groups or organizations. The
network through which investment flowed to Manchurian industry became more
complicated with the creation of the Industrial Bank in 1936 and the formation of Mangyō in 1937. The creation of the Industrial Bank added another
layer to Manchoukuo's financial system while the establishment of Mangyō,
a holding company, had similar layering effects on the corporate structure.

The year, 1939, has been chosen to illustrate the channels through
which capital flowed to Manchurian industry during the Manchoukuo Period.
This routing can best be shown diagramatically. Figure 8 traces the flow
of funds to Manchoukuo corporations engaged in mining, manufacturing,
transportation and communications in 1939. The corporations covered are

FIGURE 8: THE ROUTING OF CAPITAL TO MANCHOUKUO INDUSTRY IN 1939

unit: yen millions

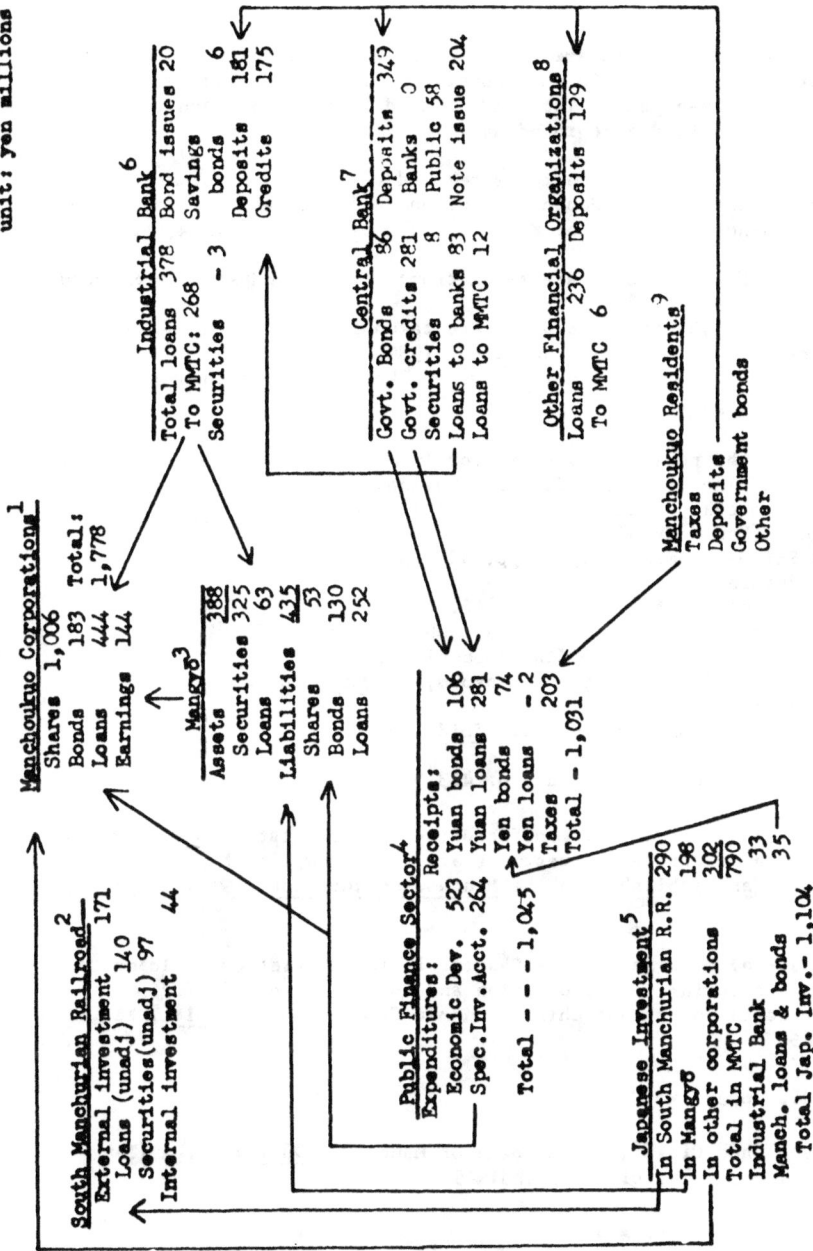

Manchoukuo Corporations[1]

Shares	1,006	Total:
Bonds	183	1,778
Loans	444	
Earnings	144	

Mangyo[3]

Assets	388
Securities	325
Loans	63
Liabilities	435
Shares	53
Bonds	130
Loans	252

South Manchurian Railroad[2]

External investment 171
Loans (unadj) 140
Securities (unadj) 97
Internal investment 44

Industrial Bank[6]

Total loans	378	Bond issues	20
To MMTC	268	Savings	
Securities	-3	bonds	6
		Deposits	181
		Credits	175

Central Bank[7]

Govt. Bonds	86	Deposits	349
Govt. credits	281	Banks	0
Securities	8	Public	58
Loans to banks	83	Note issue	204
Loans to MMTC	12		

Other Financial Organizations[8]

| Loans | 236 | Deposits | 129 |
| To MMTC | 6 | | |

Manchoukuo Residents[9]

Taxes
Deposits
Government bonds
Other

Public Finance Sector[4]

Expenditures:		Receipts:	
Economic Dev.	523	Yuan bonds	106
Spec.Inv.Acct.	264	Yuan loans	281
		Yen bonds	74
		Yen loans	-2
		Taxes	203
		Total -	1,031
Total - -	1,045		

Japanese Investment[5]

In South Manchurian R.R.	290
In Mangyo	198
In other corporations	202
Total in MMTC	790
Industrial Bank	33
Manch. loans & bonds	35
Total Jap. Inv.-	1,104

Notes to Figure 8

[1] Corporations covered are those in the series compiled in Chapter II. Figures on increases in funds available for investment by component type are those presented in Table 13. The difference between the total and other figures is due to rounding.

[2] Total external investment has been adjusted for investment outside the sectors under study. South Manchurian Railroad Data are taken from: Ōkurashō (Japanese Ministry of Finance), op. cit., Appendix 4, p. 543.

[3] Data on Mangyō assets are taken from: "Heavy Industry in Manchoukuo", op. cit., p. 70.
Data on Mangyō paid-up capital are taken from: Dairen Shōkōkaigisho (Dairen Chamber of Commerce), op. cit., 1939.
Data on Mangyō bonds and loans were taken from: Manchoukuo Yearbook, 1942, op. cit., p. 296.

[4] Data on the public finance sector in Manchoukuo were taken largely from the following article: Susumu Kurazono, "Tenkanki no Manshūkoku Zaisei," (Manchoukuo Public Finance at a Turning Point), Manshū Keizai Kenkyū Nenpō (Yearbook of Manchurian Economic Studies), Tokyo: South Manchuria Railway Company, 1941, pp. 401-432.
Expenditures:
Industrial Development: Ibid., p. 410.
Special Investment Account: Northeast China Economic Commission, op. cit., XIX, Appendix 5.
Total Government Expenditures: Kurazono, op. cit., p. 410.
Receipts:
Yuan and yen bonds and borrowings: Ibid., p. 420
Taxes: Ibid., p. 415.
Total Government Revenue: Ibid., p. 413.

[5] MMTC refers to mining, manufacturing, transportation and communications. Data on Japanese investment are those compiled by the General Affairs Board and published in the Manchoukuo Yearbook, 1942, op. cit., pp. 290-1291.

[6] Industrial Bank Data: See Chapter II for statistics on loans to mining, manufacturing, transportation and communications (MMTC).
Other data: Northeast China Economic Commission, op. cit., XIX, Appendix 15.

[7] Ibid., Appendix 10.

[8] Manshū Chūō Ginkō (Central Bank of Manchou), Jūnenshi . . (Ten Year history . .), op. cit., Appendix 9.

[9] No statistics are available.

those included in the series on corporate finances in Chapter II. As
the final users of these funds, these concerns form the apex of Figure 8.
During 1939 a total of yen 1,778 million was made available to these firms
of which yen 1,006 million resulted from increases in shares outstanding,
yen 183 million from bonds, yen 444 million from loans and yen 144 million
from the retention of earnings.

The ultimate sources of the investment funds included in Figure 8 were
the Japanese investor and Manchoukuo residents and these two groups are
indicated at the base of the diagram. Intermediary institutions such as
the banking system, the public finance sector and Mangyō enter into the
diagram between the corporations, the final users of the funds and the
individuals with whom the funds originated.

In 1939, total Japanese investment in Manchoukuo amounted to yen
1,104 million. Yen 790 million of this amount was invested in corporations
engaged in mining, manufacturing, transportation and communications. Of
this amount, yen 290 million was invested in the South Manchurian Railroad,
yen 198 million in Mangyō and yen 302 million in other corporations. An
additional yen 68 million went into the purchase of Manchoukuo government
bonds.

During the same year the South Manchurian Railroad received yen 290
million from Japanese investors, the Railroad invested yen 44 million in
activities internal to the Company and yen 171 million outside the Company.
Of this latter amount, 59% took the form of loans and 41% the form of
shares. The 1939 figures indicate that the Railroad was financed exclusively by Japanese funds in that year.

Mangyō liabilities increased by yen 435 million of which bonds
provided yen 130 million; shares, yen 53 million; and loans 252 million.

Japanese investors put up yen 198 million and absorbed all bonds issued that year. Not enough is known about the financing of Mangyō by Manchoukuo institutions. Some Mangyō bonds and shares were bought by the public finance sector and carried in the Government budget as an expenditure item of the Special Investment Account. The Industrial Bank also bought Mangyō bonds and certainly extended some loans to the holding company. During 1939, Mangyō in turn invested yen 389 million in affiliated concerns with purchases of shares accounting for 84% and loans the remaining 16%.

The banking system was crucial in financing the government sector. The Central Bank loaned large amounts to the Manchoukuo Government and was the most important holder of Manchoukuo government bonds. The banking system assisted the Government to this extent by increasing the amount of currency in circulation, accepting deposits and the sale of bonds by the Central Bank and the Industrial Bank. In 1939, currency circulation rose by yen 204 million, an amount equivalent to 56% of the Central Bank's increase in holdings of government bonds and credits extended to the government.

In 1939, total government expenditures on all aspects of the economy amounted to yen 523 million. Yen 264 million of this amount was listed under the Special Investment Account of the budget and it is only this amount which can be considered as making a direct contribution to the sectors under study. In 1939, total government expenditures amounted to yen 1,045 million and receipts yen 1,031 million. Taxes accounted for only 20% of government receipts while the increase in government bonds and credits amounted to yen 459 million or 45% of government receipts in 1939.

The reader used to the budgetary practices in the United States will be puzzled at the source of the remaining 35% of government receipts in

Manchoukuo. Manchoukuo budgetary practices were modelled after those in Japan. The budget is divided into a General Account (Ippan Kaikei) and a Special Account (Tokubetsu Kaikei) which consists of a number of individual special accounts. The General Account corresponds to a current account out of which the more normal costs of government administration are paid while the Special Account corresponds roughly to a capital account. Expenditures and receipts are distributed among the General and the Special Account. Thus, the 35% of government receipts not accounted for by taxes or increases in government bonds and credits outstanding, consists of other revenue items listed under the General Account and in individual accounts of the Special Account, such as the operating receipts of the Army Clothing Factory. On the other hand, the expenditures listed under the special account for the Army Clothing Factory consisted of payments made in order to operate the factory.[1] Thus, it is difficult to gauge what net contribution to government revenues, if any, was made by receipts carried under this special account. Receipts arising out of dividends paid to the Government for its holdings of stock in Manchoukuo corporations would of course constitute net additions to government revenues.

The methods used by the Government to finance the deficit were highly inflationary. The government bonds sold to the banking system in Manchoukuo formed the basis for further extensions of credit. The Central Bank absorbed yen 86 million of government bonds and credits extended to the Government by the Central Bank rose by yen 281 million in 1939. The price rises resulting from these fiscal policies imposed an additional tax on

---

[1]Such enterprises operated exclusively for and by the government were not included in the series constructed in Chapter II. Since these factories were not incorporated units, they do not appear in the statistics on incorporated businesses in Manchoukuo. It has not been possible to include these enterprises in this study.

TABLE 15

THE RELATIVE IMPORTANCE OF DIFFERENT INSTITUTIONS IN SUPPLYING INVESTMENT FUNDS FOR MANCHURIAN MINING, MANUFAC- TURING, TRANSPORTATION AND COMMUNICATIONS IN 1939

(unit: yen millions)

Increase in investment funds, 1939		yen 1,778 million	100%
Contribution made by:	Japan 790	44%	
	Manchoukuo Government .. 264	15%	
	Industrial Bank 265	15%	
	Central Bank 20		
		2%	
	Other Banks 6		
	Retained Earnings 144	8%	
	TOTAL	yen 1,489 million	84%

Difference attributable to investment of resident individuals:

	yen	289 million
		16%

———

Source: Data taken from Figure 8

the population in the form of inflation. The Hsinking cost of living
index rose from 125 in 1938 to 159 in 1939 and 216 in 1940 or by 73%
during the two latter years.[2]

Manchoukuo residents who formed part of the base of the diagram
constructed in Figure 8 made contributions to the expansion of industry
other than the involuntary loss of real income through inflation. These
contributions took the form of the payment of taxes, most of which were
of the excise type and the accumulation of deposits at the base of the
credit structure. Manchoukuo residents may also have held Manchoukuo
government bonds and participated in the expansion of industry more
directly through the purchase of corporate shares and bonds.

Unfortunately, there is no general breakdown of corporate shares and
bonds by domestic ownership categories. However, by inference, one can
obtain an approximate idea of the importance of the individual Manchoukuo
resident as an investor. The yen 1,778 million increase in funds available
to Manchoukuo enterprises for investment in 1939 have been disaggregated in
Table 15. If the yen 289 million arrived at in Table 15 is a reasonable
estimate of the direct contribution of individuals resident in Manchoukuo,
then their contribution to funds made available for investment in the
four sectors under study accounted for only 16% of the total in 1939.

Section 2: Japanese and Manchoukuo Investment in Mining, Manufacturing,
Transportation and Communications, 1932-1944.

Numerous estimates of Japanese investment in the area have been made
but only those of the Manchurian General Affairs Board and that presented

---

[2] 1938, and 1939 prices: Manshū Chūō Ginkō (Central Bank of Manchou),
Manshū (oroshiuri) Bukka Nenpō (Yearbook of Manchurian Wholesale Prices),
Hsinking, 1939.
1940 prices: Oriental Economist, XII, No. 3 (March, 1945), Statistical Appendix.

by the Northeast China Economic Commission are compiled on an annual basis
in sufficient detail for this study.[3] Generally speaking, the series
compiled by the General Affairs Board has been used for the years through
1940, as this series takes repatriation into account. The statistics
presented in the Northeast China Economic Commission publication are gross
figures but they have been used for 1941 through 1944 as no other annual
figures as available.

With the exception of 1935, 1936 and 1941, when Manchoukuo investment
fell off sharply causing the ratio of Japanese investment to rise, Japan
provided 41% to 61% of total investment in these sectors. The range was
somewhat narrower and lower during the years 1937 through 1942 when aside
from 1941, it consisted of 36% to 48%. While Japanese investment made an
important contribution to the financing of Manchoukuo capital growth, the
Japanese contribution to funds flowing directly into the economic sectors
under discussion was matched by investment funds collected within the area
except in 1934, 1935 and 1941.

In view of the priority given to mining, manufacturing, transportation
and communications by the Japanese war effort, the flow of resources from
Japan concentrated on these sectors of the economy and accounted for at
least 66% of total Japanese investment during 1932-1944. Japanese investment in Manchoukuo National Bonds and the bonds issued by the Industrial
Bank of Manchou must also have contributed to the expansion of the four
sectors under study. Of the yen 8,698 million Japanese investments in
Manchoukuo between 1932 and 1944, yen 960 million was invested in Manchoukuo Bonds or loans and yen 204 million in the Industrial Bank. The total

---

[3]The statistics compiled by the Manchurian General Affairs Board for
1932-1940 are available in the Manchoukuo Yearbook, 1942, op. cit., pp.
290-291. Those of the Northeast China Economic Commission are available
in Economic Encyclopedia of the Northeast, Vol. XIX: Money and Banking
in Northeast China, Appendix 2.

TABLE 16

TOTAL INVESTMENT IN MANCHURIAN MINING, MANUFACTURING, TRANSPORTATION

AND COMMUNICATIONS AND THE RELATIVE SHARE OF JAPAN AND MANCHOUKUO

(unit: yen 1,000)

	I Total Capital Available	II Japanese Investment	I-II Manchoukuo Investment	II/I Percentage of Japan
1931	16,686	N.A.	N.A.	N.A.
1932	134,700	65,000	69,700	48%
1933	184,287	90,064	94,223	49%
1934	335,867	206,000	129,867	61%
1935	366,361	350,840	15,521	96%
1936	321,931	249,656	72,275	78%
1937	653,547	268,174	385,373	41%
1938	618,301	225,637	392,664	36%
1939	1,777,727	789,666	988,061	44%
1940	1,754,892	702,507	1,052,385	40%
1941	1,215,109	820,219	394,890	67%
1942	1,641,431	783,096	858,335	48%
1943		597,450		
1944		598,343		

Sources: Total Capital: Chapter II
          Japanese Investment: See Appendix II

of these items accounts for 13% of aggregate Japanese investment and
along with the yen 5,747 million of Japanese investment in the four
sectors accounts for 79% of aggregate Japanese investment.[4]

The inclusion of all retained earnings in Manchoukuo investment
could constitute a downward bias in estimating the ratio of Japanese
investment to total investment. Theoretically, the portion of profits
retained, accruing from the use of factors of production provided by
Japan should be attributed to Japan and be included in the Japanese
investment total. The apportionment of these retained earnings between
Japanese and Manchoukuo investment posed several theoretical problems.
The simplest solution would have been to divide the retained profits
according to Japanese holdings of corporate bonds and shares as a proportion of the total. Data on the structure of the ownership of corporate
bonds and shares are available for some sectors in some years but they
are inadequate for consistent treatment of retained earnings throughout
the period according to this method.

Furthermore, such treatment of retained earnings would add little
to this chapter. It can be argued that instead of retaining a portion
of earnings, all could have been paid out and those accruing to Japanese
interests flowed back to Japan. Total funds available for investment
would then have been correspondingly lower. However, the ownership of
shareholders' equity was never a consideration in setting the pay-out
ratio of firms. Moreover, any earnings retained accrued from the profit
of operations conducted in Manchoukuo and capital was but one of the
factors of production involved.

---

[4]See Appendix II on Japanese Investment.

There were foreign investments other than Japanese. Total foreign investment was estimated at yen 2,295 million in 1930[5] of which yen 1,617 million or 70% was Japanese, yen 590 million or 26% was Soviet, yen 40 million or 2% British, yen 26 million or 1% American, and the remaining 1% French, Swedish and Danish. Soviet interests in the Chinese Eastern Railroad accounted for yen 450 million or 76% of Soviet investment. In March 1935, the Soviet Union agreed to sell its railroad interests to Manchoukuo thus greatly reducing non-Japanese foreign investment in the region. The organization of an oil monopoly in April of 1935, resulted in the gradual withdrawal of foreign interests in this sector where the major portion of American and British capital had been invested. As the period wore on, non-Japanese foreign investment was gradually repatriated. Since the non-Japanese foreign contribution to annual net investment in Manchoukuo was if anything negative and total non-Japanese foreign investment so small, it is not treated here in any detail.

The literature on Manchoukuo industrialization generally credits Japan with providing all capital, producers' goods and skilled personnel. The growth of Manchurian industry is pictured as the outgrowth of a tremendous transfer of resources from Japan throughout the period. Little if any credit for the increases in production and productive capacity is ever attributed to local resources. Japan's economic contribution was certainly crucial and in the absence of Japanese strategic considerations, the growth of mining, manufacturing, transportation and communications would have been much slower. Nevertheless, close to half the investment funds in Manchoukuo mining, manufacturing, transporation and communications

---

[5]John R. Stewart, op. cit., p. 82.

originated within the region.

There are no time series available providing statistics on total annual domestic investment in the Manchoukuo economy or any sector of it. Annual data on the investment activities of the more important institutions such as the South Manchurian Railroad, Mangyō and the Manchoukuo Government are available for most years but it is not always possible to segregate the contribution made by domestic investment to the investment activities of these organizations. The only way to arrive at annual figures concerning Manchoukuo's share of investment in the sectors under study is to deduct Japanese investment from total investment. The direction of any bias arising from the use of this method is not known. It is not possible to weigh the relative effect of omissions, errors, and double counting.

The residual attributed to Manchoukuo investment in Table 16 is plotted in Figure 9. Annual domestic investment was at the yen 70 million level in 1932 and 94 in 1933, rose to yen 130 million in 1934, fell off to yen 15 million in 1935, reached a level of yen 72 million in 1936 and then climbed steadily and steeply to yen 988 million in 1939 and yen 1,052 million in 1940. In 1941, domestic investment declined drastically to yen 395 million and recovered to a level of yen 858 million in 1942, the last year for which domestic investment has been estimated. If the 1932 level of annual domestic investment is used as a base of 100, the index for the peak year, 1940, is 1,503.

The amount of domestic investment was far more volatile than that forthcoming from Japan. The profile of Japanese investment increased continuously through 1941 after which it turned down. By contrast, domestic investment falls off sharply in 1935, is stabilized at a high

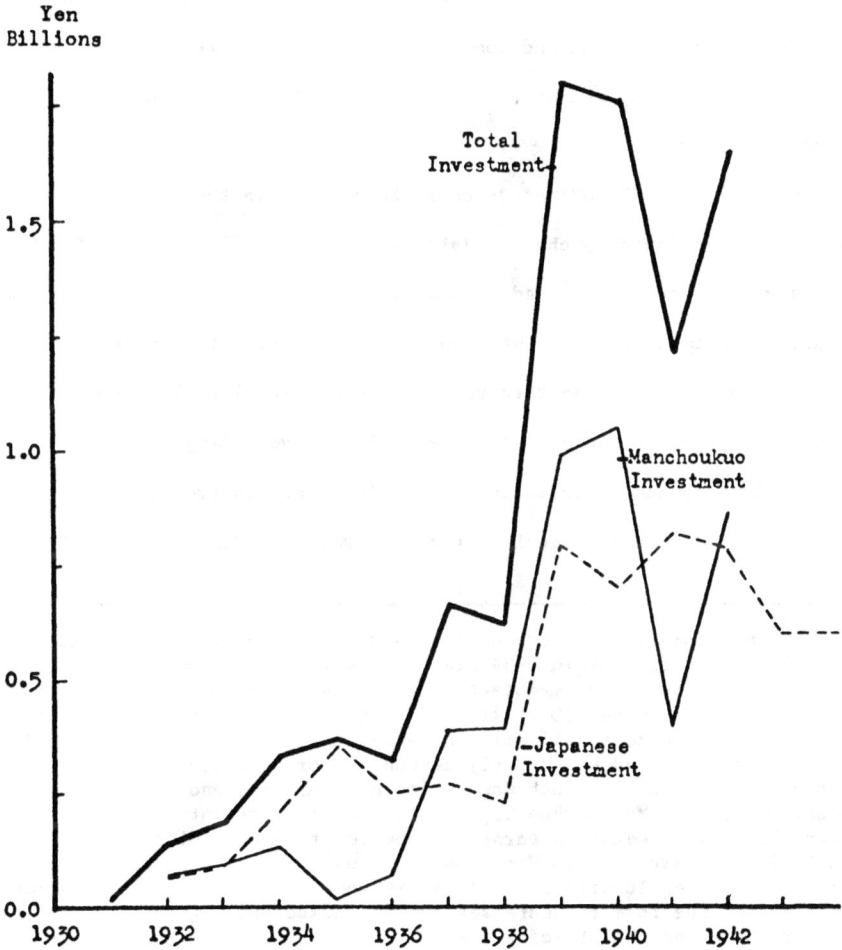

FIGURE 9

TOTAL INVESTMENT IN MANCHURIAN MINING,

MANUFACTURING, TRANSPORTATION AND COMMUNICATIONS

AND THE RELATIVE SHARE OF JAPAN AND MANCHOUKUO, 1931-1944

All data are in current prices.
Sources: As in Table 16

rate only during 1939 and 1940 and then declines abruptly in 1941.[6]

The importance of the South Manchurian Railroad as a channel for Japanese investment guaranteed a measure of stability to Japanese investment. The Railroad was so important in the economy that it was in a position of influence and its investment activities could be said to have a life of their own. In Table 17, Japanese investment in mining, manufacturing, transportation and communications has been reclassified according to the following channels: The South Manchurian Railroad; Mangyō; and other corporations.

During 1932-1937, 69% of Japanese investment in the four sectors was absorbed by the South Manchurian Railroad. After 1937, when the first five year plan was inaugurated and Mangyō established, the proportion of Japanese investment flowing into Manchoukuo via the Railroad dropped to about 43% through 1942 and then rose to the 60% level in 1943 and 1944 due to the sharp drop in Japanese investment in Mangyō. Mangyō accounted for 17% to 28% of Japanese investment in the four sectors from 1938 through 1942, and only 8% of Japanese investment flowed into Mangyō during 1943.

---

[6]The reasons for the decline in Manchoukuo's contribution to funds available for investment in 1935 are not clear. Total funds made available for investment in mining, manufacturing, transportation and communications in 1935 rose by only yen 30 million. Manchoukuo's contribution declined by yen 114 million to yen 16 million while that of Japan rose by yen 145 million over 1934, and was largely accounted for by a loan of yen 75 million extended to the South Manchurian Railroad and another loan of yen 60 million to help Manchoukuo buy out the Soviet interest in the Chinese Eastern Railroad. Retained earnings amounted to yen 33 million and have been implicitly ascribed to Manchoukuo. Thus, if absolute Manchoukuo investment was yen 16 million in 1935, it would follow that disinvestment took place in the form of decreases in Manchoukuo holdings of shares, bonds or the extension of loans.

The situation in 1941 is explained by the stabilization of loans at roughly the 1940 level. In the series on investment funds by component type, the statistics on loans after 1940 were based on Manchoukuo banking data and the figures available on loans made by Mangyō to subsidiaries. Thus, the series on loans represented a domestic source of capital and accordingly any change in the contribution made by loans was reflected in the amount of Manchoukuo investment.

TABLE 17

THE CHANNELS THROUGH WHICH JAPANESE INVESTMENT IN MANCHOUKUO
MINING, MANUFACTURING, TRANSPORTATION AND COMMUNICATIONS FLOWED

(unit: yen 1,000)

	South Manchu-rian Railway	Mangyō	Other Cor-porations	Total
1932	65,000 100%			65,000 100%
1933	81,200 90%		8,864 10%	90,064 100%
1934	166,000 81%		40,000 9%	206,000 100%
1935	246,340 70%		104,500 30%	350,840 100%
1936	133,205 53%		116,451 47%	249,656 100%
1937	161,000 60%	10,000 4%	97,174 36%	268,174 100%
1938	77,344 34%	38,500 17%	109,793 49%	225,637 100%
1939	290,391 37%	197,635 25%	301,640 38%	789,666 100%
1940	343,950 49%	194,642 28%	163,915 23%	702,507 100%
1941	345,000 42%	199,800 24%	275,419 34%	820,219 100%
1942	360,000 46%	170,000 22%	253,096 32%	783,096 100%
1943	376,558 63%	45,000 8%	175,892 29%	597,450 100%
1944	360,489 60%		237,854 40%	598,343 100%

Source: See Appendix II on Japanese Investment in Manchoukuo

The remainder of Japanese investment in mining, manufacturing, transportation and communications flowed into the area via other corporations. During the plan period these concerns accounted for a greater portion of Japanese investment than Mangyō and less than the South Manchurian Railroad.

The reliance on the South Manchurian Railroad as an economic link between Japan and Manchoukuo is easily understood. Since its inception in 1905, the Railroad had relied largely on the flotation of bonds to finance its capital expenditures. Aside from some earlier issues floated in London, these bonds issues had been absorbed by the capital market in Japan. Consequently, the Railroad had established itself as a sound outlet for investment funds and had ready access to Japanese financial resources. The attitude of the Japanese investor towards the Railroad continued to be favorable despite the actions of the Kwantung Army in narrowing the scope of Railroad activities and replacing uncooperative personnel.

In conclusion, between 1932 and 1942, yen 9,004 million was available for investment in the sectors selected for study. Yen 1,343 million was forthcoming during 1932-1936 when Japan provided 62% and Manchoukuo, 38%. Investment was gradually stepped up during the plan period. Between 1937 and 1942, yen 7,661 million was mobilized for investment and Japan and Manchoukuo each provided 50%. During the period as a whole, Japan's contribution amounted to 52% and Manchoukuo's to 48%.

Actual Japanese investment in these sectors just met that planned while domestic investment exceeded anticipated Manchoukuo investment. The economic plans drawn up for 1938-1942 called for a Japanese contribution of yen 4,003 million while the actual amount forthcoming was yen

3,978 million or 99.4% of that anticipated. The goal for Manchoukuo
investment was set at yen 2,606 million during the same years. Yen 3,686
million was forthcoming within Manchoukuo so the goal for domestic investment was exceeded by 41%. The plans had also called for investment by
third countries through 1941 when these hopes were finally abandoned.
Assistance by Germany and Italy was mostly in the form of trade agreements
or credits extended to the Central Bank of Manchou rather than direct
investment in Manchoukuo concerns and the burden of supplying the funds
anticipated from third countries was assumed by Manchoukuo rather than
Japan.

Section 3: The Institutions through which Capital Flowed to Manchoukuo
Mining, Manufacturing, Transportation and Communications.

This section concerns the relative importance of various institutions
active in promoting investment in the sectors covered in this study. It
will appear that government or government-controlled organs were of overwhelming importance in promoting investment and that the private investor
resident in Manchoukuo whatever his nationality played a minor role.
However, in the absence of an independent series on private Manchoukuo
investment residuals must be relied on and they do not command great confidence.[7] The South Manchurian Railroad, Mangyō, the banking system and
the Manchoukuo Government budget were the institutions of primary importance
in channelling funds to Manchurian mining, manufacturing, transportation

---

[7]It has not been possible to allocate all capital flowing into
Manchoukuo corporations engaged in mining, manufacturing, transportation
and communications among the various institutions promoting the flow.
Series can be constructed for the South Manchurian Railroad, Mangyō,
the Government, the banking system or the corporations themselves but
they can not be made mutually exclusive. Furthermore these statistics
may not be comparable to the series on total funds available for investment presented in Chapter II.

and communications. Good data are available on the finances and investment activity of the South Manchurian Railroad and Mangyō. It has been
assumed that the data on these two institutions are mutually exclusive.[8]

In assessing the role played by the South Manchurian Railroad the
growth in Railroad liabilities has been traced. In analyzing the
increase in funds available for investment by the South Manchurian Railroad Company, no adjustment has been made for changes in the security
holdings of the Railroad. In this connection inquiry is limited to the
Railroad itself and accordingly no double counting has occurred. This
approach overstates the Railroad's role in relation to the four sectors
under study in proportion to the Railroad's Security holdings in activities other than mining, manufacturing, transportation and communications.
Yet this approach is the most comparable to the series on total investment funds available to the four sectors.[9]

In Table 18 data are presented on the annual amount of funds
available for investment by the South Manchurian Railroad and the ratio
of this amount to the total for the four sectors as estimated in Chapter II.

---

[8]The Railroad had been functioning since 1905 as a quasi investment trust in Manchuria. When Mangyō was established in 1937, its stock
was subscribed by the Manchoukuo Government and the Nissan interests in
Japan. Bonds issued by Mangyō were not bought by the Railroad. At
least the breakdown of Railroad holdings of securities in 1945 makes no
mention of Mangyō bonds.

[9]The series on total funds available for investment compiled in
Chapter II, included the annual increases in paid-up capital, corporate
bonds of the Railroad and loans made to the Railroad, plus annual earnings retained, minus the net change the security holdings of the Railroad
in other corporations. The amount of Railroad security holdings in each
year was deducted from the corresponding figure on the paid-up capital
of the Railroad since these securities had already been counted as paid-
up capital of the issuing corporations.

TABLE 18

TOTAL INVESTMENT FUNDS FOR THE FOUR SECTORS AND THE AMOUNT OF FUNDS

AVAILABLE TO THE SOUTH MANCHURIAN RAILROAD FOR INVESTMENT, 1931-1944

(unit: yen 1,000)

	Total Funds for Four Sectors	South Manchurian Railroad				
		Increase in Paid-up[a] Capital	Increase in Bonds	Retained Earnings[b]	Net Japanese Loans to R.R.	Total Funds for the Railroad
1931	16,686 100%		19,475	-1,945		17,530 105%
1932	134,700 100%	25,000	73,475	37,017		135,492 101%
1933	184,287 100%	79,821	-11,677	13,293		81,437 44%
1934	335,867 100%	38,231	159,775	13,197		211,203 63%
1935	366,361 100%	37,747	114,775	13,474	75,000	240,996 66%
1936	321,931 100%	34,203	124,775	11,143	-75,000	95,121 30%
1937	653,547 100%	74,050	20,775	31,446	84,000	210,271 32%
1938	618,301 100%	20,000	153,875	27,973	-59,000	142,848 23%
1939	1,777,727 100%	40,000	215,165	31,395	25,000	311,560 18%
1940	1,754,892 100%	120,000	237,355	25,606	-5,000	377,961 22%
1941	1,215,109 100%	100,000	270,755	14,586		385,341 32%
1942	1,641,431 100%	130,000	236,305	20,130		386,435 24%
1943		130,000	255,655	20,631		406,286
1944		183,792	385,305	32,163		601,260

[a]Refers to the annual increase in the paid-up capital of the South Manchurian Railroad. No adjustment was made for the Railroad's holdings of securities in other companies.

[b]Retained earnings were calculated from balance sheet data by subtracting the amount of dividends paid from given year profits.

TABLE 18 (cont'd)

Sources:

Total Funds for Four Sectors: As in Table 13 of Chapter II.

Increase in Paid-up Capital:
    1930:   South Manchurian Railroad, Second Report on Progress
                  in Manchuria to 1930 (Dairen, 1930), p. 104.

    1930-1931,   Ōkurashō (Japanese Ministry of Finance), op. cit.,
    1940-1944:   Appendix 3.

    1933-1936:   Tōyō Keizai K.K. (East Asia Economic Company), Kabu-
                  shiki Kaisha Nenkan (Yearbook of Stock Companies),
                  Tokyo, 1938, p. 387.

    1937-1939:   Dairen Shōkō Kaigisho (Dairen Chamber of Commerce),
                  op. cit., 1937, 1938, 1939.

Increase in Bonds:
    Ōkurashō (Japanese Ministry of Finance), op. cit., Appendix 1.

Retained Earnings:
    Ibid., Appendix 10.

Net Japanese Loans to the Railroad:
    Manchouko Yearbook, 1942, op. cit., pp. 290-291.

During the pre-plan years, 1931-1936, yen 782 million or 58% of total
funds available for investment in Manchurian mining, manufacturing,
transportation and communications was channelled through the South Manchurian Railroad. During the plan years from 1937 through 1942, total capital
available to the four sectors increased markedly to yen 7,661 million and
the relative share of the Railroad declined to 24% or yen 1,810 million.
Except for dips in 1933, 1936 and 1938, funds available for investment by
the Railroad increased steadily from 1931 through 1944 when a peak of yen
601 million was reached.

    In Figure 10 funds available to the South Manchurian Railroad for
investment have been plotted against the total amount of investment funds

FIGURE 10

TOTAL INVESTMENT FUNDS FOR MINING, MANU-

FACTURING, TRANSPORTATION AND COMMUNICATIONS AND THE

INVESTMENT FUNDS OF THE SOUTH MANCHURIAN RAILROAD, 1931-1944

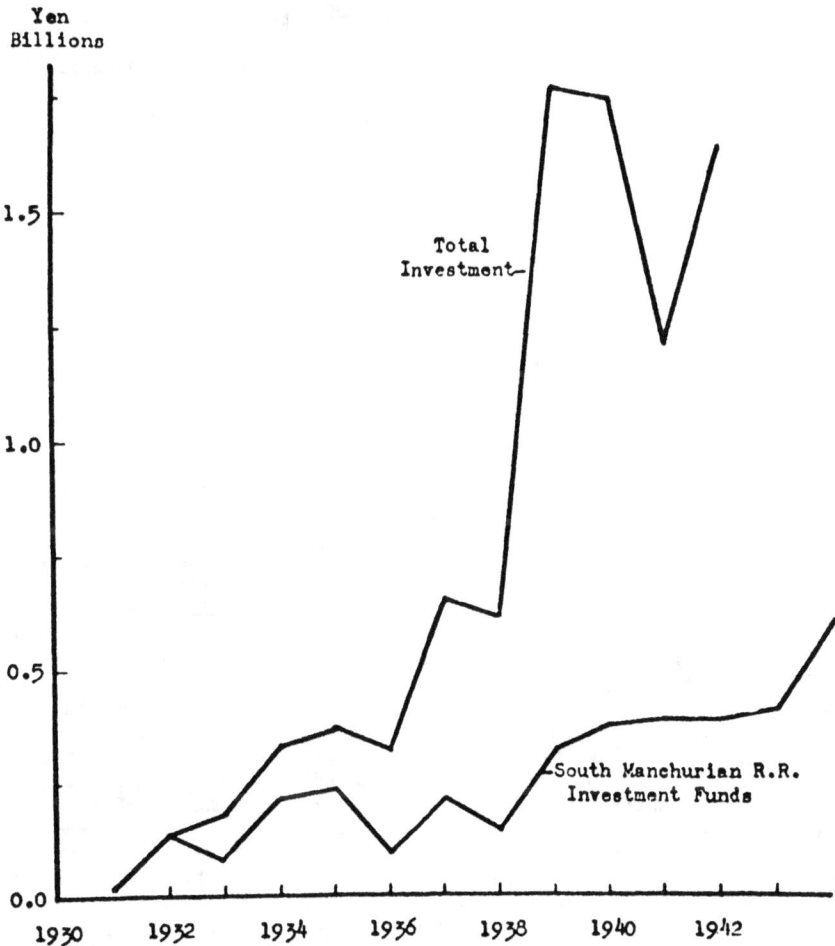

All data are in current prices.
Sources: As in Table 13 and Table 18

available to the four sectors during 1931-1942. The profile of the balance
sheet data is very smooth after 1936 in comparison with the angularity of
the graphic representation for total funds available. Generally speaking,
the South Manchurian Railroad relied on an orderly program of bond flotation as its main source of funds. Except for 1933 and 1937, the net
increase in debentures outstanding greatly exceeded increases in paid-up
capital outstanding or the amount of earnings retained.

Mangyō was the other institution important in promoting investment.
Statistics on Mangyō investment in Manchoukuo are presented in Table 19.
As would be expected of a holding company, equity investment was far more
important than loan investment. In 1938, Mangyō investment in Manchoukuo
amounted to yen 250 million.[10] During 1939 and 1940, the years of peak
annual increment to funds available for investment, Mangyō contributions
were yen 388 million and yen 526 million or respectively 22% and 30% of

---

[10]This figure amounts to 40% of total funds available for investment
and is excessive. Originally, the paid-up capital of Mangyō was set at
yen 450 million, half of which was to be provided by the Manchoukuo Government and the other half by the Nissan interests in Japan. A large part of
the contribution of the Manchoukuo Government took the form of industrial
assets already in existence. Some of these concerns, such as the Showa
Steel Works had originally been under the aegis of the South Manchurian
Railroad. Others, had been sponsored by the Manchoukuo Government. Some
of the Railroad's shares in concerns destined for control by Mangyō may
have been bought out by the Government and then transferred to Mangyō along
with Government shares. Such transfers show up as a net increase in
Mangyō investments in Manchoukuo when in effect only a shift in the claims
on existing plant is involved. The total compiled for the four sectors
records net increases in paid-up capital and bonds outstanding and does
not reflect mere shifts in the ownership of corporate shares and bonds.
Thus, whatever portion of Mangyō investment represented shifts in the
ownership of outstanding shares and bonds rather than increases in the
same overstates the contribution of Mangyō to funds available for investment in the four sectors in any given year. These transfers of industrial
assets were heaviest in 1937 and 1938 so this factor is of much less
importance after 1938.

the total. During the years 1938-1942, Mangyō provided yen 1,781 million or 25% of the total. Thus, Mangyō's contribution exceeded that of the South Manchurian Railroad during these years.[11]

TABLE 19

MANGYŌ INVESTMENT IN LOANS TO

AND SHARES OF MANCHURIAN SUBSIDIARIES, 1938-1944

(unit: yen millions)

| | Loans | | Shares | | Total |
	Total Outstanding	Annual Increase	Total Outstanding	Annual Increase	Annual Increase
1938	3	3	247	247	250
1939	66	63	572	325	388
1940	170	104	994	422	526
1941	471	301	1,027	33	334
1942	495	24	1,286	259	283
1943	629	134	1,735	449	583
1944 (July 1)	695	66	1,892	157	223

Source: "Heavy Industry in Manchoukuo," op. cit., p. 71.

---

[11]That is, Mangyō's gross financial contribution exceeded the financial contribution of the South Manchurian Railroad. However, the latter amount is much closer to a net figure. The Mangyō figure includes the transfer of claims on existing assets discussed in footnote 9. It also includes any double counting existing between Industrial Bank of Manchou loans and loans made by Mangyō in Manchoukuo (See Chapter II, Section 3). Any double counting among these loans is included in the series on total investment as well as those for Mangyō and Industrial Bank investment so the effect of the double counting is diluted in calculating the share of Mangyō.

FIGURE 11

MANGYŌ INVESTMENT AND TOTAL FUNDS

AVAILABLE FOR INVESTMENT IN MINING, MANUFAC-

TURING, TRANSPORTATION AND COMMUNICATIONS, 1931-1943

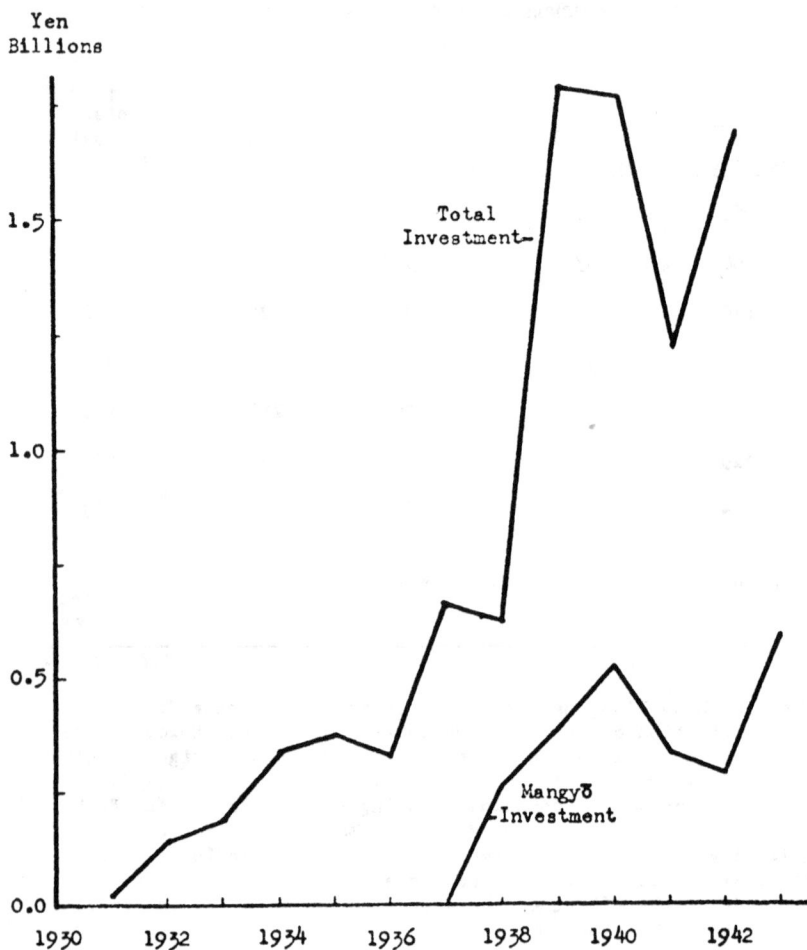

All data are in current prices.
Sources: As in Table 13 and Table 19

In Figure 11, Mangyō investment in subsidiaries in Manchoukuo is shown along with total funds available for investment in mining, manufacturing, transportation and communications. The Mangyō figure dips sharply in 1941 and 1942 when it amounted to respectively yen 334 million and yen 283 million. Two factors were responsible for this decline. Industrial Bank loans were reduced in 1941 to dampen inflation and Mangyō would logically have followed suit in decreasing investment. Furthermore, the tightening of credit by the Industrial Bank affected Mangyō's ability to invest since the Bank purchased Mangyō bonds and extended credit to the Company. The thorough-going reorganization of Mangyō in 1941 which required the Company to give up its Japanese interests in return for greater control over the conduct of its business in Manchoukuo was another factor. This reorganization forced the Company to rely more heavily on Manchoukuo sources of capital for investment. Initially, this reduced the resources made available to Mangyō for investment but by 1943, the last full year for which data on Mangyō investment are available, a peak of yen 583 million was invested in Manchoukuo by the holding company.

Table 20 sets forth the amounts of investment funds provided by institutions. Columns I through VI are explained in the notes to the table and have been adequately discussed elsewhere. Column VII, the summation of Columns II through VI and Column VIII, a residual comprising the difference between Column I, total investment, and Column VII, are of greatest interest. It is not possible to construct an independent series for investment by private individuals in Manchoukuo so the residual in Column VIII must be used to approximate the contribution of private domestic investment.

This residual represents investment by the Government and the Industrial

TABLE 20: TOTAL FUNDS AVAILABLE FOR INVESTMENT AND THEIR SOURCES, 1931-1944

(unit: yen 1,000)

	I Total	II S.M.R. Invest. Resources	III Mangyo	IV Bank Loans	V Retained Earnings Less SMR	VI Jap. Inv. ex.Mangyo & SMR	VII Total II,III IV,V,VI	VIII Residual I - VII	IX Gov.Share Holdings in Corp.	X Spec. Invest Account	XI Indus. Bonds	XII Bank Shares	
1931	16,686 100%	17,530 105%			838 5%		18,368 110%	-1,682 -10%					1931
1932	134,700 100%	135,492 101%			1,242 1%		136,734 102%	-2,034 -2%					1932
1933	184,287 100%	81,437 44%		-2,775 -2%	10,186 6%	8,864 5%	97,712 53%	86,575 47%					1933
1934	335,867 100%	211,203 63%		9,561 3%	17,384 5%	40,000 12%	278,148 83%	57,719 17%		15,944			1934
1935	366,361 100%	240,996 66%		-1,563 -.5%	19,644 5%	104,500 29%	363,577 99%	2,781 1%		10,908			1935
1936	321,931 100%	95,121 30%		4,427 1%	22,558 7%	116,451 36%	238,557 74%	83,374 26%		23,875			1936
1937	653,547 100%	210,271 32%		39,562 6%	40,826 6%	97,174 15%	387,833 59%	265,714 41%		144,691		30,234	1937
1938	618,301 100%	142,848 23%	250,000 40%	82,074 13%	65,699 11%	109,793 18%	650,414 105%	-32,113 -5%		447,059		6,124	1938
1939	1,777,727 100%	311,560 18%	388,000 22%	287,417 16%	112,961 6%	301,640 17%	1,401,578 79%	376,149 21%	88,978	263,564		-3,502	1939
1940	1,754,892 100%	377,961 22%	526,000 30%	416,752 24%	107,495 6%	163,915 9%	1,592,123 91%	162,769 9%	77,102	319,549		-8,795	1940
1941	1,215,109 100%	385,341 32%	334,000 27%	-275,766 -23%	76,776 6%	275,419 23%	795,770 65%	419,339 35%	26,352	288,304	460,000	3,143	1941
1942	1,641,431 100%	386,435 24%	283,000 17%	65,776 4%	46,049 3%	253,096 15%	1,034,356 63%	607,075 37%	41,565	219,768	60,000	5,248	1942
1943		406,286 24%	583,000	328,953		175,892			-37,518	236,787	342,240	14,830	1943
1944		601,260	223,000	1,200,556		237,854			377,940	383,625	1,143,980	-8,575	1944

TABLE 20 (cont'd)

Notes and Sources:

Column

I. Total: Represents total annual increase in funds available for investment in Manchurian mining, manufacturing, transportation and compiled in Chapter II. See Table 13.

II. S.M.R. Earnings and Liabilities: This item represents the annual increment in funds available to the South Manchurian Railroad for investment without any adjustment for the activities of the Railroad outside the sectors under study. The figure constitutes the annual increase in the paid-up capital of the Railroad, the annual increase in Railroad bonds outstanding, the annual increase in loans made to the Railroad and the annual retention of earnings by the Railroad.

Sources: As in Table 18.

III. Mangyō: Annual increase in Mangyō investment in Manchoukuo subsidiaries. See Table 19 for sources and more information.

IV. Bank Loans: Includes annual increment in loans extended by private banks, the Central Bank of Manchou and the Industrial Bank of Manchou. For sources and further information see Table 12.

V. Retained Earnings less S.M.R.: Represents the annual contribution of retained earnings to total funds available for investment. The global estimates for retained earnings in the four sectors as compiled in Chapter II were taken and the corresponding figure for the retained earnings of the South Manchurian Railroad deducted as the latter has been included in Column II on the financial resources available to the Railroad.

Sources: Global estimates of retained earnings: See Table 8.
Earnings retained by the South Manchurian Railroad: See Table 18.

VI. Japanese Investment less Mangyō and SMR: This series represents the annual amount of funds forthcoming from Japan other than the amount flowing through the South Manchurian Railroad and Mangyō. The last mentioned two amounts have been implicitly included in Column II on the South Manchurian Railroad and Column III on Mangyō. Column VI corresponds to the series on "Other Corporations" in Table 17. See Table 17 and Appendix II for sources.

TABLE 20 (cont'd)

Notes and Sources:

IX. Government Share Holdings in Corporations: This series represents the annual increase in Government investment in the shares of Manchoukuo special and semi-special corporations engaged in communications, mining and manufacturing. Investment in Mangyo and the South Manchurian Railroad is not included. This series is available for 1938-1944 so annual increments may be computed for 1939-1944. No data have been found for the earlier years though the Government most certainly invested in Manchoukuo enterprises.

Source: Northeast China Economic Commission, op. cit., XIX, Appendix 21.

X. Special Investment Account: This series refers to the amount allocated to the Special Investment Account in the Special Account of the Manchoukuo Government budget. The figures for 1934-1942 refer to actual expenditures made through the Account while those for 1943-1944 constitute budgetary estimates.

Source: Northeast China Economic Commission, op. cit., XIX, Appendix 5.

XI. Industrial Bank Bonds: Annual increment in holdings of corporate debentures by the Industrial Bank.

Source: Northeast China Economic Commission, op. cit., XIX, Appendix 15.

XII. Industrial Bank Shares: This series refers to the annual change in Industrial Bank holdings of securities.

Source: As for Column XI.

Bank in companies engaged in mining, manufacturing, transportation and communications, as well as investment by private individuals in Manchoukuo.[12] It is difficult to find any stability or pattern in the ratio of the residual to total investment funds available to the four sectors. The residual ranges from minus 10% of total funds available in 1931 to plus 47% in 1933. The negative ratios indicate either statistical errors and inconsistencies such as over-lapping coverage between items making up Column VII or disinvestment on the part of private individuals.

Columns IX, X, XI and XII have been included in Table 20 because they help isolate the portion of the residual attributable to private domestic investment. Column IX refers to net increases in government holdings of shares in mining and communications and excluded government purchases of Mangyō shares and investment in the South Manchurian Railroad. Thus, Column IX does not duplicate any of the series included in the residual. Unfortunately, the same does not apply to Columns X, XI and XII. Column X refers to government investments made through the Special Investment Account of the Special Account of the government budget. These expenditures probably included the series listed in Column IX and though the four study sectors must have predominated, investment in activities outside the scope of this study were also included. Column XI probably largely reflects Industrial Bank holdings of Mangyō bonds which are implicitly included in Column III.

It is difficult to evaluate the residual for the years prior to 1936 as much of the data consists of estimates.[13] However, the negative

---

[12]Mangyō and the South Manchurian Railroad excluded.

[13]Prior to 1934, no breakdown of paid-up capital by industry is available and a similar breakdown of corporate debentures was first published in 1935.

residuals obtained for 1931 and 1932 are undoubtedly due to disinvestment during the depression years. In 1936, the residual amounted to yen 83 million or 26% of total funds available. 1937 when the residual amounted to 41% or yen 266 million, was the first year the expenditures of the Special Investment Account amounted to a substantial sum, namely yen 145 million. It was also the first year during which the Industrial Bank was operative and the Bank purchased yen 30 million in securities. If half of these amounts were invested in the four sectors under study, the residual attributable to the private sector would have been around 27%.

The residual in 1938 was negative, minus 5%, because much of the yen 250 million Mangyō investment in Column III represented a shift in the ownership of claims on existing assets rather than new investment. Assuming that the Manchoukuo Government share of Mangyō's initial capitalization consisted entirely of claims held against existing assets, the value of the residual would rise to 31%.[14] If one further assumes that one-half of the Special Investment Account and Industrial Bank purchases of shares represented investment in the four study sectors, Mangyō excluded, the residual would fall sharply to around 14%.[15]

In 1939, the residual attributable to private investment is 147

---

[14] Amounting to yen 225 million, and to be deducted from Mangyō's share in Column III and from Column VII in arriving at the adjusted residual of 31%.

[15] The 14% figure was calculated in the following manner: one-half of (Column X minus yen 225 million investment in Mangyō) plus one-half of the increase in Industrial Bank shares was deducted from Column VII after Column VII has been adjusted for yen 225 million of Mangyō investment. The decision to adjust for one-half of the expenditures of the Special Investment Account and Industrial Bank holdings of shares was an arbitrary one. Judging from the structure of the various Special Accounts of the Government budget, the author is sure that at least this amount was invested in the four study sectors.

if one again assumes that half of the Special Investment Account expenditures and Industrial Bank investment in shares flowed into the four study sectors. The 1940 residual calculated on the same basis falls to 0.5% which is unduly low, and may be because of double counting among the Columns in Table 20. Investment in 1940 amounted to yen 1,755 million, roughly the same level as in 1939, but the amount accounted for by Column II through VI rises by almost yen 200 million with conspicuous increases in Mangyō investment and Industrial Bank loans.

In 1941 and 1942, South Manchurian Railroad investment resources, Mangyō investment, Industrial Bank loans, retained earnings, and Japanese investment outside Mangyō and the Railroad accounted for respectively 65% and 63% of total investment in Manchurian mining, manufacturing, transportation and communications. After adjustment for half the amounts listed under the Special Investment Account (Column X) and Industrial Bank holdings of shares (Column XII), the residual unaccounted for is 23% for 1941 and 31% for 1942. Part of the rise in this residual in 1941 and 1942 over previous years was undoubtedly due to the purchase of corporate debentures by the Industrial Bank listed under Column XI. But purchases of Mangyō bonds by the Industrial Bank must have been heavy in 1941 and they were implicitly included in Column III on Mangyō investments so no adjustment was made for Industrial Bank holdings of corporate debentures.[16]

----

[16]No corporate bonds are listed as assets on the balance sheets of the Industrial Bank of Manchou prior to 1941 when they rose from zero to yen 460 million. Mangyō bonds must have formed an important part of this increase. After the reorganization of Mangyō in 1941, the sale of Mangyō bonds shifted from Japan to Manchoukuo and the Industrial Bank would have naturally assumed a large portion of them.

In summary, the residuals not accounted for by Columns II through
VI and the adjustment for Special Investment Account expenditures and
Industrial Bank investment in corporate shares were as follows:

	Residual listed in Column VIII	Column VIII Adjusted for half of Column X and XII
1936	26%	22%
1937	27%	27%
1938	14%	14%
1939	16%	14%
1940	5%	0.5%
1941	32%	23%
1942	34%	31%

These residuals merely suggest the level of private domestic investment during these years. Data prior to 1936, are largely based on crude
estimates and not to be relied on. Data available for the years of the
economic plans are more reliable when taken by institutional component but
the danger of duplication between the series on institutional components
is very real. In the author's opinion, the share of funds made available
from private domestic sources during the plan years was at a peak in 1937
(27%) and declined thereafter to around 15%.

No distinction has so far been made between investments by Japanese
living in Manchoukuo and by other residents. Since Japanese controlled
the modern sector,[17] through political as well as economic means, Japanese

---

[17]The "modern" sector has been defined empirically in this study as
consisting of the firms in the four study sectors, which operated as
incorporated units. It has been assumed that Industrial Bank loans to
mining and manufacturing were limited to incorporated units. Investment
in firms in the modern sector was controlled by the Manchoukuo authorities
by administrative means and through the banking system and the special
companies.

living in Manchoukuo would be more likely to invest in the four study
sectors than would native Manchurians or Chinese residents in Manchoukuo.
But aside from political considerations, there were economic deterrents
to the investment of native capital[18] in the modern sector.

According to a study by the Central Bank of Manchou on the financial
background of 225 businesses operated by native capital in 1938 with total
assets amounting to yen 35 million,[19] the disparity between the rate of
profit in native businesses and profit and dividend rates in the modern
sector was sufficient to discourage the investment of native capital in
the modern industrial sector. Two profit rates are cited for businesses
operated by native capital, the ratio of profits to original investment
and the ratio of profits to total capital used. Comparable measures of
profit are available for the modern industries; the ratio of profits to
paid-up capital which is somewhat equivalent to the former, and the ratio
of profits to total capital[20] in use which is the same for both types of
industries. The profit rates for the foodstuffs and textile industries

---

[18]"Native capital" is the term used to refer to the traditional or
non-modern sector of the economy owned by Manchurians and Chinese. The
Manchoukuo Government was not able to effectively control investment within
the "native" sector. Firms in the native sector were generally small scale
unincorporated business units.

[19]Shuzui Hajime, "Dochaku Shihon to Shikkin Dōin," (Native Capital
and the Mobilization of Capital Funds), Manshū Keizai Kenkyū Nenpō
(Yearbook of Manchurian Economic Studies), Tokyo: South Manchuria Railway
Company, 1941, pp. 291-353.

[20]The term "total capital" includes all sources of funds. In the
case of an incorporated business unit the following items are included:
shareholders' equity (paid-up capital outstanding, reserves, and carry-
over from the previous year), long term, short term, and miscellaneous
debts outstanding. In the case of the traditional business units operated
by native capital the term refers to the amount of original investment
by the operator, any profits retained, and credits received.

in 1938 are compared below:[21]

	Ratio of Profits to Original Capital or Paid-up Capital	Ratio of Profits to Total Capital Used	Dividend Rate
Foodstuffs			
Native Sector	122%	16%	
Modern Sector	20%	6%	9%
Textiles			
Native Sector	224%	23%	
Modern Sector	26%	10%	11%

The great disparity in the profitability of the two types of business needs explanation. If profits are considered a measure of efficiency, the incorporated units must have been less efficient than the concerns operated by native capital on a much smaller scale and using more traditional methods of production. The disparity may, however, be attributed to a divergence between money and real costs in the concerns operated by the native entrepreneur. Household labor was important in the concerns operated by native entrepreneurs and the wages paid to household labor are notoriously low. In the relatively labor intensive foodstuffs and textile industries, the difference in wage costs may explain the profit differential between the modern and native sectors. But in the absence of statistics on relative costs in the two sectors, this argument cannot be substantiated.

The underrevaluation of factor costs in small scale, traditional, owner-operated enterprises is common in under-developed areas. The only costs that enter into the native capitalists' calculation of profits are

---

[21]Shuzui Hajime, op. cit., p. 326 for the profit rates in native industries. Dairen Shokō Kaigisho (Dairen Chamber of Commerce), op. cit., 1938, for profit rates in modern industries.

money costs and only the money costs directly attributable to the operation of the business. If the native entrepreneur had included imputed
money costs and calculated real costs, the profit rates of native
industries would have been substantially lowered. But as long as the
calculations of profits made by the native entrepreneur exceeded those of
firms operating in the modern sector, regardless of the theoretical comparability of the respective profit rates, the native businessman would
not consider investing in the modern sector.

In rural areas and the smaller cities, the money lender rather than
the operator of a business had access to large enough lots of capital to
make investment in the modern sector practicable. In 1935, the interest
rate charged on loans made by pawn shops was 2.5% per month and the rate
probably did not fall below this level during the Manchoukuo Period.[22]
Thus, the money lender would not have invested in the modern sector where
the return on capital was relatively low. Furthermore, the native
capitalist had a very short time horizon in mind when investing. He was
less interested in the growth in the market value of his investment than
in the amount of money return on his investment over a year or an even
shorter period and he looked with disfavor on being geographically
separated from his investment. Even if the native lender ruled out
investment in a firm in which he had no part in the management, the
Manchoukuo authorities hoped to induce resident Manchurians and Chinese
to deposit their funds in banks or other financial intermediaries which
would in turn finance industries given priority by the Government. But
the interest rate on time deposits was set at 4.7% in 1936, hardly enough

[22]Northeast China Economic Commission, op. cit., XIX, p. 137.

to attract large deposits.[23]

Thus by deduction, it appears that the native sector contributed little to the residual attributed to domestic private investment. However, simply attributing the investment to the modern sector begs the question of which individuals did the investing. It is easy to define the modern and native sector in terms of the firms operating in each sector, but it is very difficult to establish criteria for distinguishing the individual investors aside from the tautalogical one of the sector in which they invested. The best one can do is to make certain deductions concerning individuals investing in the modern sector. The private investor in the modern sector was certainly a city dweller and likely a Japanese. As of 1940, 6 million people, or 13% of Manchuria's population lived in eighteen cities of 50,000 or more people.[24] In 1940, there were slightly over one million Japanese in Manchoukuo and the Kwantung leased territory and most of them lived in cities.[25] Sixty percent of the Japanese were engaged in mining, manufacturing, transportation, commerce or had government jobs compared to 12% of the Chinese population.[26] Income

---

[23]This rate prevailed until at least 1941. See Manshū Chūō Ginkō (Central Bank of Manchou), Jūnenshi . . (Ten Year History . .), op. cit., p. 128.

[24]U.S. Department of Commerce, Bureau of the Census, The Population of Manchuria, International Population Statistics Reports, Series p-90, No. 7, U.S. Government Printing Office, Washington, D.C., 1958, Appendix Table 1, p. 63. The figure cited in the text includes the population of Dairen-Port Arthur.

[25]Ibid., p. 41.

[26]Northeast China Economic Commission, op. cit., XIX, p. 285, gives the following data on individual deposits in Manchoukuo financial organizations as of June 1944:

levels in these occupations would have been above those for agriculture, forestry or domestic work and frequently salaries paid to Japanese were higher than those paid to Chinese in similar positions. So the Japanese population was in a better economic position to invest. However, even more important was the political and psychological affinity of the Japanese population to the Manchoukuo Government and the planned sector.

	Number of Depositors	Amount of Deposit
Manchurian	7.4 million 81%	yen 757 million 34%
Japanese-Korean	1.7 million 19%	yen 1,432 million 65%
Other	---	---
Total	9.1 million 100%	yen 2,222 million 100%

These figures probably do not include Kwantung Leased Territory. The number of Manchurian depositors greatly exceeds that of Japanese and Koreans as would be expected in an area where the ratio of Japanese and Koreans to total population was 5% in 1940. It is difficult to obtain comparable figures for urban population though in 1940, Japanese may have accounted for as much as 18% of the population of cities over 50,000. However, deposits of Japanese and Koreans accounted for 65% of the total and each deposit averaged yen 842 while the average deposit of Manchurians was yen 102.

CHAPTER IV

AN EVALUATION OF MANCHURIAN INDUSTRIAL INVESTMENT,

THE AMOUNT AND ITS SOURCES

The evaluation of Manchurian industrial investment requires that the
figures compiled be given some frame of reference. Just what does the
estimated yen 9 billion invested in Manchurian mining, manufacturing,
transportation and communications really mean? How do the series compiled
on the basis of current prices compare with those in constant prices? Do
the statistics compiled on financial resources available for investment
differ significantly from actual financial investment? And most important
of all, can the data compiled be related to estimates of national income
or gross national product? Only after these questions are answered, can
one assess the effectiveness of Manchurian industrial investment during
the period under study.

The equipment goods price index compiled by the Central Bank of
Manchou is here selected as the deflator for the series on funds available
for investment compiled in current prices in Chapter II. The equipment
goods index is a weighted arithmetic average of the prices of twelve goods
basic to the construction of industrial facilities and 1933 is the base
year of the index.[1]

---

[1]The twelve goods and their weights are as follows:

Cement	(2)	Iron Bars	(4)	Galvanized Plate	(2)
Red Bricks	(3)	Sheet Iron	(4)	Corrugated Plate	(2)
Timber	(6)	Iron Plate	(4)	Paint	(1)
Pig Iron	(6)	Nails	(2)	Concrete Blocks	(1)

Source: Minami Manshū Tetsudō (South Manchuria Railway), Manshū ni
okeru Bukka Chōsa narabi ni Shisū Kōsei no Genjō (Manchurian Price Studies
and the Construction of Price Indices), 1941, p. 57.

TABLE 21

Total Investment in Current and Constant Prices

	Total Inv. Current Prices	Total Inv. 1933 Prices	Total Inv. 1937 Prices
1933-1942	8,869	5,653	7,878
1937-1941	6,020	3,568	4,970

Source: This table is an abstract of Table 22. See Table 22 for the sources of the data.

The application of the equipment goods price index as a deflator with 1933 as the base year, reduces the amount of investment during 1933-1942 to 64% of the amount of the series in current prices. In terms of 1933 prices, annual investment grows from yen 184 million in 1933 to a peak of yen 1,084 million in 1939 or by 589% compared to the 966% increase registered by the current price series. Thus, despite all the pressures towards inflation, the rise in the prices of equipment goods after 1933 nullified only one-third of the amount of funds available for investment as measured in current prices.

The author has also recomputed the equipment goods index using 1937 as the base year and deflated the series in current prices accordingly in order to focus attention on trends during the first five year plan. This computation raises the series in 1937 prices markedly over that of the 1933 price series due to the sharp price rises of iron and steel products during 1937.[2] Total investment from 1933 to 1942 in the sectors under

---

[2]The price index for metals in Manchuria rose sharply during 1938 and 1939 and then fell with the imposition of price controls:

1933	100	1937	162
1934	91	1938	212
1935	94	1939	156
1936	93		

Source: Manshū Chūō Ginkō (Central Bank of Manchou), Manshū Bukka Nenpō (Yearbook of Manchurian Prices), Hsinking, 1939, pp. 4-6.

TABLE 22

TOTAL INVESTMENT IN MANCHURIAN MANUFACTURING, MINING, TRANSPORTATION AND COMMUNICATIONS, 1933-1942:

IN CURRENT PRICES, 1933 PRICES AND 1937 PRICES

Year	Total Investment Current Prices	Equipment Goods Price Index 1933:100	Equipment Goods Price Index 1937:100	Total Investment 1933 Prices	Total Investment 1937 Prices
1933	184,287[a]	100[b]	72[c]	184,287[d]	255,954[e]
1934	335,867	94	67	357,305	501,294
1935	366,361	94	68	389,745	538,766
1936	321,931	92	66	349,925	487,774
1937	655,847	139	100	470,178	653,547
1938	618,301	175	125	353,315	494,640
1939	1,777,727	164	118	1,083,979	1,506,548
1940	1,754,892	173	124	1,014,388	1,415,235
1941	1,215,109	188	135	646,334	900,080
1942	1,641,431	203	146	808,586	1,124,267
1943		232	167		
1933-1942	8,869,453			5,658,042	7,878,105

[a] Total Investment in Current Prices: As in Table 13.

[b] Equipment Goods Price Index, 1933:100. Manshū Chūō Ginkō (Central Bank of Manchou), Manshū Bukka Shirabe (Survey of Manchurian Prices), Hsinking, 1943, p. 10.

[c] Equipment Goods Price Index, 1937:100. The equipment goods price index with 1933 as the base year was recomputed with 1937 as the base year.

[d] Total Investment, 1933 Prices: Total investment in current prices deflated by the equipment goods price index with 1933 as the base year.

[e] Total Investment, 1937 Prices: Total investment in current prices deflated by the equipment goods price index with 1937 as the base year.

study in 1937 prices is yen 7,878 million or 89% of the series based on current prices for 1933-1942 and yen 4,970 million or 83% of the series based on current prices during 1937-1941. While the series in 1933 prices is a better measure of real investment during the Manchoukuo Period, the series based on 1937 prices is a better indicator of the success of the economic planners in reaching the goals set for financial investment in the plans.

The annual increase in the fixed assets and inventories of Manchurian manufacturing, mining, transportation and communications is the measure selected to estimate the portion of financial resources available for investment actually invested in expanding plant, equipment and inventories. Inventories are defined as stocks and goods in process while fixed assets include land, buildings, machinery, patent and leasing rights less depreciation.[3] The procedure for estimating the annual increase in total fixed assets and inventories is the same as that used in constructing the series on retained earnings in Chapter II.

During 1938-1942, the growth in fixed assets and inventories of Manchurian manufacturing, mining, transportation and communications amounted to yen 6,098 million in current prices or 87% of the yen 7,007 million available for investment. Thus, during this five year period, the Manchoukuo economic authorities were successful in translating their financial plans for investment into real terms.

As would be expected, the level of investment maintained during the period of the economic plans had a cumulative effect on the annual growth of fixed assets. There is an inevitable time lag between the time investment

of work in progress is also included. Theoretically, land
ng rights should be excluded from this analysis of fixed
hey do not constitute capital formation.

TABLE 23: ESTIMATED ANNUAL INCREASE IN THE FIXED ASSETS AND INVENTORIES OF MANCHURIAN MANUFACTURING, MINING, TRANSPORTATION AND COMMUNICATIONS, 1938-1942

(unit: yen 1,000)

Industry		1938	1939	1940	1941	1942	1938-1942
Group A:							
Chemicals	FA[a]	69,277	239,810	744,923	367,630	378,105	
Metals & Machinery	Inv[b]	53,440	59,285	216,916	79,805	240,264	
Lumber & Wood							
Ceramics							
Group B							
Textiles	FA	24,149	24,094	116,753	1,542	140,885	
Foodstuffs	Inv	47,393	19,225	112,144	-27,639	109,866	
Electricity & Gas	FA	52,045	46,874	88,610	93,074	240,470	
	Inv	5,593	10,449	12,600	8,211	-35,558	
Mining	FA	101,342	288,127	340,010	244,015	693,736	
	Inv	29,353	86,996	71,370	49,138	91,338	
Transportation	FA	44,828	50,755	143,463	103,307	163,790	
	Inv	36,567	10,750	21,339	11,440	-132,310	
Communications	FA	9,977	19,674	26,871	34,895	23,032	
	Inv	1,569	3,693	9,732	4,789	-25,020	
Total Fixed Assets		301,618	669,334	1,460,630	844,463	1,640,018	4,916,063
% Total Investment		49%	38%	83%	69%	100%	70%
Total Inventories		173,915	190,398	444,101	125,144	248,580	1,182,138
% Total Investment		28%	11%	25%	10%	15%	17%
Total Fixed Assets & Inventories		475,533	859,732	1,904,731	969,607	1,888,598	6,098,201
% Total Investment		77%	48%	108%	79%	115%	87%

[a] FA is an abreviation for fixed assets.   [b] Inv is an abreviation for inventories.

TABLE 23

(cont'd)

Estimation Procedure:

The annual increase in the fixed assets and inventories of Manchurian manufacturing, mining, transportation and communications was estimated on the basis of data contained in the series published by the Dairen Chamber of Commerce and the Central Bank of Manchou on the business results of Manchurian enterprises. Among the data contained in these series are figures on the value of total fixed assets and inventories of firms included in the series. The annual increases in fixed assets and inventories for the firms included in these series were calculated for 1938-1942 by subtracting the amounts for one year from those of the previous year. The annual growth in total fixed assets and inventories was then estimated by increasing the figures on the annual increase in the fixed assets and inventories of firms included in the series on business results in proportion to the ratio of total sector paid-up capitalization to the paid-up capital of firms included in the series. This procedure is the same as that used in estimating retained earnings in Section 2 of Chapter II.

Sources of Data:

Sample study data on paid-up capitalization, total fixed assets and inventories:

1937-1941: Dairen Shōkō Kaigisho (Dairen Chamber of Commerce), op. cit., 1937-1941.

1942: Manshū Kōgyō Ginkō (Industrial Bank of Manchou), Manshū Jigyō Kaisha Seiseki Bunseki (Analysis of Business Results of Manchurian Enterprises and Companies), Hsinking, 1942.

Data on industry-wide paid-up capitalization: As in Table 3, and Table 4.

Total investment: Table 13.

funds are received and the time they are transformed into productive plant and equipment. The ratio of the growth in fixed assets to total investment funds available rose from 49% and 38% in 1938 and 1939 to 83% in 1940, 69% in 1941 and 100% in 1942. Once the net change in inventories is taken into account, the difference between the increase in fixed assets and inventories and total investment funds is explained by cash balances, working capital, and the inevitable errors, omissions, and incomparabilities between the two series.

The author has little confidence in the statistics which purport to measure Manchoukuo national income for selected years so the net rate of investment calculated is treated as a rough guess.[4] Nothing is known of the methodology used in compiling these figures which forces one to guess at the prices which have been used in the weighting system. The author has assumed that since 1937 is the first year for which a national income estimate is available, it is the base year and 1937 prices have been used in weighting the production data used.

If the national income figures in Table 24 are valid and if realistic assumptions have been made concerning base year prices, the net rate of investment in Manchurian mining, manufacturing, transportation and communications was 24% in 1937, 30% in 1939, but in 1941 the combined effect of price increases and a decline in absolute investment lowered the rate to 12%. In view of the amount of Japanese investment, it is not possible to say that the rate was "high" or "low." However, one can estimate the

---

[4]In addition to the national income data presented in Table 24, there is a two volume abstract of Manchurian national income in 1941; Manshū Chōsa Kikai Rengōkai (Institute for Manchoukuo Studies), Manshūkoku Kokumin Shotoku Chōsasho (Study of Manchoukuo National Income), 1943. This study presents estimates of Manchoukuo national income based on distributive shares but the volume available gives no information on methodology. This study estimates total national income at yen 6,807 million in 1941 compared to the estimate of yen 7,235 million presented in Table 24.

TABLE 24

THE ESTIMATED RATE OF NET INVESTMENT IN MANCHURIAN
MANUFACTURING, MINING, TRANSPORTATION AND COMMUNICATIONS
FOR SELECTED YEARS

(unit: yen millions)

	1937	1939	1941	1943
Manchurian National Income	2,709	5,070	7,235	9,634
Total Investment in MMTC[a] in 1937 Prices	654	1,507	900	
Estimated Rate of Investment[b] in MMTC	24%	30%	12%	
Domestic Investment in MMTC in 1937 Prices	385	837	293	
Estimated Rate of Domestic Investment in MMTC	14%	17%	4%	

[a]MMTC refers to manufacturing, mining, transportation and communications.

[b]This investment rate is defined as a net rate because the series
on total funds available for investment in Manchurian mining, manufacturing, transportation and communications compiled in Chapter II is net of
depreciation. However, the investment series is net of depreciation in the
bookkeeping sense only and may not be a net series in theoretical terms
as depreciation allowances in Manchuria were very low.

Sources: National Income: Mimeographed document in the Suitsu Collection
at Hitotsubashi University in Tokyo. The original source is
quoted in the document simply as "Seifu no Chōsa ni yoru"
(Survey by the Manchoukuo Government).

Total Investment in 1937 Prices: Table 22

Domestic Investment in 1937 Prices: Table 16
Series in current prices deflated by equipment goods price index.

rate of domestic investment in these industries at 14% in 1937, 17% in 1939 and 4% in 1941. In 1937 and 1939, the domestic investment rates were certainly high for a predominantly agricultural country while the 4% figure for 1941 was more usual.

Whatever the exact rate of industrial investment, it is clear that investment in Manchoukuo industry during the first five year plan was maintained at a high level. Chapter III outlined the institutions through which investment to Manchoukuo industry flowed. However, institutions such as Mangyō, the South Manchurian Railroad and the Industrial Bank were intermediaries rather than the primary source of the funds so the question of the real source of the investment remains unanswered. One must determine whether a flow of goods from Japan to Manchoukuo accompanied the flow of financial resources as well as where the real source of domestic investment lay.

According to Chapter III, Japan provided 52% of the investment in the sectors under study during 1932-1944. Throughout this period, Manchoukuo maintained a large import surplus in the merchandise trade account with Japan and these amounts represent a transfer of real resources from Japan to Manchoukuo. Between 1938 and 1944, Manchoukuo's commodity trade account with Japan was as follows:[5]

	Imports	Exports	Import Surplus	
1938	993	417	577	
1939	1,541	521	1,019	
1940	1,860	469	1,391	unit: yen millions
1941	1,509	485	1,024	current prices
1942	1,526	593	933	
1943	1,511	694	818	
1944	1,100	707	393	

---

[5]Northeast China Economic Commission, op. cit., XIX, pp. 313-318.

During 1936, Manchoukuo imports of metals machinery and tools, and
chemicals amounted to yen 218 million or 41% of imports from Japan.[6]
After 1937, the statistics on the composition of merchandise trade are
both unreliable and incomplete because shipments of many strategic goods
were kept secret. Begining in 1940, the only data available for Manchoukuo imports by commodity refer to imports from all countries but this is
not a serious defect because Japan was the chief supplier of producer
goods at this time. In 1940, total imports of machinery, metals and
metal products, and chemicals amounted to yen 571 million or 31% of
imports from Japan and in 1943, to yen 366 million or 33% of imports from
Japan.[7] These imports were certainly intended for use in Manchurian mining,
manufacturing, transportation and communications and they corresponded to
87% of Japanese investment in these sectors in 1936, 81% in 1940 and 61%
in 1943.

The overwhelming importance of investment emanating from Japan or the
official or semi-official organs of the Manchoukuo Government is an established fact.[8] In the author's opinion, these sources accounted for over
70% of investment in 1937 and their share may have risen to the 85% level

---

[6]Minami Manshū Tetsudō (South Manchuria Railway), Manshū Keizai Tōkei
Nenpō, Showa 10/11 (Yearbook of Manchou Economic Statistics for 1935 and
1936), Dairen, pp. 159-171.

[7]Northeast China Economic Commission, op. cit., Vol. XX: Trade (Mukden,
1948), pp. 61-62. This reference gives data on commodity trade for 1940-
1943.

[8]Investment statistics indicate that the South Manchurian Railroad
was financed almost exclusively by Japanese investment. Mangyō on the other
hand was financed by Japanese investment, the Special Investment Account of
the Manchoukuo Government and the Industrial Bank. Thus, retained earnings
are the only item entering into Column VII of Table 20 on "Total Funds
Available for Investment and Their Sources, 1931-1944" which does not emanate
directly from Japanese or Manchoukuo Government investment.

TABLE 25

THE MANCHOUKUO NATIONAL DEBT,

TREASURY EXPENDITURES AND TREASURY RECEIPTS, 1932-1945

(unit: yen millions)

| | Manchoukuo National Debt[a] | | Treasury[b] Expenditures | Treasury[c] Receipts |
	Total Outstanding	Annual Increase		
1932	39		119	
1933	119	80	183	
1934	139	20	245	163
1935[d]	231	92	167	93
1936	324	93	365	224
1937	444	120	586	212
1938	704	260	980	240
1939	1,291	587	1,059	300
1940	1,773	482	1,955	418
1941	2,227	454	1,891	814
1942	2,372	645	1,815	990
1943	3,316	444	1,978	1,032
1944	3,813	497	2,741	1,413
1945			4,174	

[a]Government bond issues plus total loans to the Manchoukuo Government.

[b]Total expenditures in the general and special account of the government budget, adjusted for double counting arising out of transfers between accounts. The figures for 1932-1942 refer to actual expenditures while those for 1943 and 1944 refer to anticipated expenditures.

[c]Includes revenue from taxes, customs and monopoly profits. These items are listed under the revenues of the general account of the budget. Transfers from the special account and receipts from bond issues listed under the general account have been excluded for all years but 1941. The

figure for 1941 refers to total receipts of the general account as no
other figure was available.

dFiscal year 1935 included only six months, June 1-December 31.

Sources.

National Debt: Northeast China Economic Commission, op. cit., XIX,
                Appendix 7.

Treasury Expenditures: Ibid., Appendix 6.

Treasury Receipts:
    1934:   South Manchuria Railroad, Fifth Report on Progress . ., op.
            cit., p. 152.
    1935-
    1940:   Manchoukuo Yearbook, 1942, op. cit., p. 207.
    1941:   Northeast China Economic Commission, op. cit., XIX, Appendix
            5, item listed as the receipts of the general account.
    1942-
    1944:   Ibid., Appendix 20, item listed under Central Government,
            financial levies.

---

during the rest of the plan period.[9] The contribution of the Manchoukuo

Government certainly equalled that of the Japanese during the plan period

except possibly in 1941. The Manchoukuo Government budget and the Indust-

rial Bank of Manchou were the chief instruments of government investment

but they were both financial intermediaries.

Treasury expenditures were financed by increases in government loans

and bonds as well as by revenue from taxes, customs and monopoly profits.

Between 1937 and 1944, increases in the national debt[10] accounted for

anywhere from 18% to 55% of annual treasury expenditures. Since some

government accounts were calculated on a gross basis,[11] the ratio of the

---

[9]See Chapter III, pp. 111-118

[10]Defined here as the annual increase in Manchoukuo Government bonds
plus the annual increase in loans to the Government.

[11]See Chapter III, pp. 90-91

annual increase in the national debt to annual revenues from taxes, customs
and monopoly profits is a better measure of deficit financing than the
ratio of either of these items to total treasury expenditures. The ratio
of the annual increase in the national debt to annual government revenue
from taxes, customs and monopoly profits was as follows from 1937:[12]

1937	.57
1938	1.08
1939	1.96
1940	1.15
1941	.56
1942	.65
1943	.43
1944	.35

Thus, it is clear that deficit financing was important in all years and
that during 1938, 1939 and 1940 receipts from loans and bond sales exceeded
traditional sources of revenue.

The sale of government bonds need not be inflationary but in the
Manchurian case it was highly inflationary. The Central Bank of Manchou
assumed a large portion of Manchoukuo bonds throughout the period. The
Central Bank then sold whatever amounts it could, usually to other banks.
Few if any of the Manchoukuo bonds issued were assumed in such a way as
to absorb purchasing power. In fact, the contrary was often the case
because the government bond holdings of banks formed the basis for the
extension of credit or the purchase of corporate bonds and shares by the
banking system.

Perhaps the best overall measure of inflationary pressures in Manchoukuo is the amount of currency in circulation and the level of bank deposits.
The data on currency in circulation and deposits prior to 1936 are hard
to evaluate because it was during this period that the currency was unified

---

[12]See Table 25.

TABLE 26

CURRENCY IN CIRCULATION, BANK DEPOSITS

AND PRICE TRENDS IN MANCHOUKUO, 1932 - 1945

(unit: yen millions)

	Currency Circulation	Bank Deposits	Annual Increase in Currency & Deposits		Wholesale Prices	
			Amount	Percentage	Index	Increase
1932	152	n.a.			102	
1933	131	300			100	(-) 2%
1934	184	427	180	42%	93	(-) 7%
1935	199	505	93	15%	103	11%
1936	275	647	218	31%	106	3%
1937	330	808	216	23%	125	18%
1938	453	1,108	423	37%	150	20%
1939	657	1,876	972	62%	181	21%
1940	991	2,125	583	23%	226	25%
1941	1,317	2,886	1,087	35%	249	10%
1942	1,728	3,809	1,334	32%	268	8%
1943	3,080	5,132	2,675	48%	299	12%
1944	5,877	8,840	6,505	79%	358	20%
1945 (June)	7,709	10,062	3,054	21%	599	67%

Sources.

Currency Circulation: Northeast China Economic Commission, op. cit:, ҮIX, Appendix 10.

Bank Deposits and Price Index: Ibid., pp. 12, 20, 29.
Price index quoted is the index of wholesale prices in Hsinking compiled by the Central Bank of Manchou.

and the banking system consolidated. Therefore, the annual increases in currency in circulation and the amount of deposits reflected to a large extent the unification of the currency and the effect on prices was negligible. By 1935 and 1936, soya bean prices had returned to levels prevalent before the depression and the economy was functioning smoothly.

The launching of the first five year plan increased the need for funds and as most of the financing flowed through the banking system or arose from the Manchoukuo Government budget, the amount of currency in circulation and deposits rose steadily. During the first five year plan, annual increases ranged from 23% to 37% except for 1939 when the increase shot up to 62%. The reader will recall that 1939 was the year during which investment almost tripled over the previous year. The annual increase in currency in circulation and deposits rose steadily from 32% to 48% and then to 79% between 1942 and 1944.

The annual increase in prices between 1937 and 1940 ranged from 18% to 25% but with the institution of price controls, the economic authorities held the annual increase in official wholesale prices down to the 8% to 20% range between 1941 and 1944. Thus, prior to 1941, the annual increase in prices was substantial but less than that of currency and deposits.

Starting in 1941, the authorities held the annual increase in the prices of goods traded in official channels down to one-fourth of the rate of increase for currency and deposits. Thus, the economic authorities tried to suppress inflation. However, their failure is indicated by black market operations in the cities from 1941 onward. This activity was widespread enough for the Central Bank of Manchou to compile black market price indices which show far greater price rises than the indices based on official prices.

TABLE 27

INDICES FOR BLACK MARKET PRICES

IN HSINKING, MUKDEN, HARBIN AND BY COMMODITY GROUP

Part I

General Index of Black Market Prices in Three Cities

		Hsinking	Mukden	Harbin
1941		100	100	100
1942		142	155	164
1943		214	440	354
1944:	Jan.	638	791	703
	June	595	697	545
1945:	Jan.	1423	1646	1519
	June	2627	3054	2136

Part II

Black Market Price Indices for
Three Cities By Commodity Group, June 1945

(1941 = 100)

	Hsinking	Mukden	Harbin
Chief Grains	1997	2047	1088
Auxilliary Grains	1692	1913	1057
Seasonings	2835	4418	2712
Luxuries	4735	5188	4324
Clothing	2322	2290	2154
Fuel	1994	2125	1700
Miscellaneous	2814	3393	1917
General Average	2627	3054	2136

Source: Documents in the possession of Mr. Hasegawa, former director
of the Central Bank of Manchou.

No data are available on the quantitative importance of black market operations. Official prices were undoubtedly effective where the Government controlled the distribution of goods. Thus, the Government was in the best position to control the prices of raw materials and the finished products of heavy industry and mining where special companies of some size dominated production. Conversely, government price controls were least effective over consumers goods where great numbers of producing and distributing units were active. In fact the black market price indices are based solely on consumers goods.

Inflation certainly levied a heavy tax on the Manchoukuo population through 1941 and depending on the importance of black market transactions, this tax may have been greater in later years. The cost of living more than doubled during the first five year plan. The cost of living index for Hsinking was 100 at the end of 1936 and by the end of 1941 it had climbed to 250.[13] Wages rose during this period but not enough to offset the rise in prices. The wages paid to some occupations kept pace with the price rises in 1938 and 1939 but thereafter inflation eroded the purchasing power of the Manchurian worker.[14]

---

[13]Sources citing the cost of living index compiled by the Central Bank of Manchou:

    1936-1939: Manshū Chūō Ginkō (Central Bank of Manchou), Manshū Bukka Nempō (Yearbook of Manchurian Prices), Hsinking, 1939.
    1940-1944: Tōyō Keizai Shimpōsha, Oriental Economist (March 1945), Statistical Appendix.

[14]For wage data see:
a) The Manchoukuo Yearbook,.1942, op. cit., pp. 645-656.
b) Yoshio Sataru, "Senjitaiseika no Manjin Rodōsha no Jōtai" (Wartime Conditions of Manchurian Labor), Manshū Keizai Kenkyū Nenpō (Yearbook of Manchurian Economic Studies), Tokyo: South Manchuria Railway, 1940, pp. 364-365.
c) Yoshinobu Adachi, "Manshū Kōgyō Rōdō ni Kan suru futatsu mitsu no Kosatsu" (Two or Three Case Studies of Labor in Manchurian Manufacturing), Mantetsu Chōsa Geppō (South Manchuria Railway Monthly Studies), 1940, p. 110.

The sociology of inflation in Manchoukuo was so complicated it is difficult to identify the groups or sectors which paid most heavily for the inflationary financing of government expenditures and economic development.[15] One can only draw very broad conclusions concerning the incidence of inflation in Manchoukuo. The more dependent a group was on the money economy, the greater the impact of inflation on the group. The wage earner could escape the adverse effects of inflation only if his wages rose enough to offset price increases and this did not happen. Thus, the city dweller and the migrant laborer were adversely affected by inflation. The farmer, however, could always withdraw from the market and produce for home consumption. He would have to forego consumer goods obtained through the market but he could at least eat well. The agricultural sector could make this choice because the Manchoukuo Government made no attempt to control agricultural production directly and its controls over the distribution of agricultural products were ineffective until 1943.

During 1937-1939, the agricultural sector marketed 46% of its production, or an average of 8.2 million metric tons annually. During 1940-1942, after the institution of government controls on the distribution on farm products, the ratio of agricultural production marketed fell to 30% or 5.4 million metric tons annually. These statistics are based on transactions through official channels. One source estimates that an additional

---

[15]The standard of living of Japanese and Manchurians was different. Important cultural differences existed between the two groups and made for dissimilarities in the pattern of expenditures of a Japanese and a Manchurian in the same income group. The Japanese resident lived on a higher standard than the native Manchurian partly because he was usually at least a skilled worker and frequently belonged to the managerial class, and partly because a Japanese worker in many trades was paid wages almost double those of a Manchurian worker performing the same task. These and other factors make it difficult to determine just which groups suffered most from inflation.

2 million metric tons of agricultural products reached the market through unofficial channels during 1940-1942 and would mean that the agricultural sector sold one-fourth to one-third of production marketed on the black market.[16] Government controls on distribution were much more effective during 1943 and 1944 when the ratio of agricultural produce sold through official channels rose to 43% or an average of 8.3 million metric tons each year. However, due to an increase in production, the absolute amount retained for consumption including that marketed unofficially was 11.1 million metric tons compared to 9.7 million metric tons during 1937-1939 and the amount not consumed surely found its way to the black market.

TABLE 28

TOTAL AGRICULTURAL PRODUCTION AND THE AMOUNT

MARKETED AND RETAINED FOR CONSUMPTION, 1937-1939, 1940-1942,

AND 1943-1944

	Average Production	Quantity Marketed	Ratio Marketed	Quantity Retained	Ratio Retained
1937-1939	17,991,069[a]	8,244,562	45.8%	9,746,507	54.2%
1940-1942	18,345,739	5,422,659[b]	29.6%	12,923,080	70.4%
1943-1944	19,355,606	8,297,975[b]	42.9%	11,057,631	57.1%

[a]Production of soya beans, kaoliang, millet, maize, wheat, rice, other cereals and oil seeds in metric tons.
[b]The figures for 1940-1942 and 1943-1944 refer to amounts marketed through official channels.

Source: Northeast China Economic Commission, op. cit., III, p. 109.

---

[16]Northeast China Economic Commission, op. cit., Vol. III: Distribution of Farm Products in Northeast China (Mukden, 1948), pp. 9-10.

The agricultural sector's contribution to economic development
ng this period consisted of producing food and keeping the population
starving. Aside from contributing little directly to industrial
lopment in Manchoukuo, agriculture's indirect contribution through
luntary savings was probably far below that of the urban sector. The
lanced nature of the development and the economic controls both dis-
aged the flow of resources from agriculture to industry, and in
long run these were serious mistakes in a country with a well
loped and commercialized sector. However, the imminent world war
ed the authorities to consider only the short run and to concentrate
resources and energies on the expansion of heavy industry.

CHAPTER V

SUMMARY AND CONCLUSIONS:

THE LESSONS OF THE MANCHURIAN EXPERIENCE

The most salient features of the economy during the Manchoukuo
Period were: the planned growth of investment and production in mining,
manufacturing, transportation and communications; the importance of
institutions such as the South Manchurian Railroad, Mangyō and the
Industrial Bank; the steady infusion of Japanese capital; the great
increase in domestic investment; and pronounced inflation caused mainly
by deficit financing of government expenditures.

Between 1931 and 1942, total funds in current prices available for
investment in the four sectors totalled yen 9,021 million and annual
investment rose from yen 135 million in 1932 to a peak of yen 1,778
million in 1939, an increase of 966%. The application of the equipment
goods price index as a deflator with 1933 as the base year reduces the
amount of investment during 1932-1942 to 64% of the series in current
prices or yen 5,658 million. If the base year is shifted to 1937, investment in the four sectors amounted to yen 7,878 million or 89% of the
series in current prices. While the series in 1933 prices is the best
measure of real investment during the Manchoukuo Period, the series with
1937 as the base year, indicates the success of the economic authorities
in meeting the goals set for financial investment in the five year plans.

During this period, corporate shares accounted for 51% of additions

to investment funds, bonds for 24%, loans for 17% and retained earnings
for 8%. The relative importance of these components changed during
the period and these shifts are more readily explained by institutional
than economic factors. Paid-up capital and loans became far more important while bonds and retained earnings declined as sources of investment
funds. Paid-up capital increased in importance due to the existence of
Mangyō a holding company which financed and controlled affiliates through
purchases of their stock. Loans increased in importance due to the
lending activity of the Industrial Bank of Manchou and Mangyŏ which were
established to finance mining and manufacturing. Government control was
assured by the special company system so the Government relied heavily
on bank credit, which it considered the most flexible method of financing.
Bonds, which had always been the main source of South Manchurian Railroad
financing declined in relative importance due to the change in the
economic structure in which transportation declined in importance while
mining and manufacturing became more important. This structural shift
was the direct result of the Government's decision to give priority
to mining and manufacturing. The contribution of internal financing
fell due to the steady decline in profits after 1938 or 1939.

The development of mining, manufacturing, transportation and communications was controlled by the Manchoukuo Government but the actual
task of operating these industries was delegated to the South Manchurian
Railroad, Mangyō and the special companies. The South Manchurian Railroad
and Mangyō both functioned as investment trusts with managerial peroga-
tives and both institutions made a great contribution to development in
the planned sector during the Manchoukuo Period. The Railroad and to
a lesser extent Mangyō, attracted Japanese capital that would otherwise

not have been available to Manchoukuo economic development and both
institutions provided the managerial talent vital to transform investment
funds into operating productive capacity. Furthermore, the manufacturing
industry in Manchoukuo was relatively small, so the existence of these
institutions made it possible to enjoy some economies of scale.

Government or government controlled organs were of overwhelming
importance in promoting investment while the private investor in Manchuria, whatever his nationality, played a minor role. During 1931-
1936, the South Manchurian Railroad provided yen 728 million or 58% of
total funds available for investment in Manchurian mining, manufacturing,
transportation and communications. During 1937-1942, when the five year
plans were formulated and Mangyō organized, total capital available to
the four sectors increased markedly to yen 7,661 million and the relative
share of the Railroad declined to 24% or yen 1,810 million while the
contribution of Mangyō amounting to yen 1,781 million roughly, equalled
that of the South Manchurian Railroad.

All the factors discussed heretofore, reflect the situation in
the "modern" sector of the economy. However, in Manchoukuo the "traditional" sector far outweighted the "modern" sector in terms of the number
of people employed, exports and certainly in terms of income produced.
It is important to estimate the contribution or lack of contribution
made by the "traditional" sector. Whenever the "traditional" sector
in an underdeveloped area fails to participate directly or indirectly
in developing the " modern" sector of the economy, a colonial pattern
of economic development will prevail in which a modern economic island
will be developed apart from the surrounding native economy. This was,
in effect, the situation in Manchoukuo.

In the author's opinion, the share of funds made available from private domestic sources during the plan years was at a peak of about 27% in 1937 and declined thereafter to around 15%. The Japanese population in Manchoukuo probably contributed all of this amount. Japan controlled the "modern" sector through political as well as economic means so it is unlikely that native Manchurians or Chinese residents in Manchoukuo invested in the "modern" sector. Furthermore, there were economic deterrents to the investment of native capital in the "modern" sector. Profits in the "native" sector, at least as calculated by the entrepreneurs in that sector exceeded those of firms operating in the modern sector and the interest earned on time deposits in modern banking institutions was to low to attract native capital. Also, as inflation became pronounced, the generally speculative approach of the native businessman was strengthened. Thus, it appears that the private contribution to investment in Manchurian mining, manufacturing, transportation and communications was also drawn from the "modern" sector.

The policy of the Manchoukuo Government in favoring heavy industry above all and the methods used to expand heavy industry, worked against the modernization of the economy as a whole and long term economic growth. The most important aspect of modernization in an area such as Manchuria is increasing the flow of goods and services between the agricultural and the industrial sectors which correspond roughly to the "traditional" and the "modern" sectors. Any increase in these flows encourages the specialization of labor, implies a rise in income and and can lead to the transfer of resources from the agricultural to the industrial sector. Until this transfer of resources takes place, either through the market mechanism or direct controls, economic growth in secondary industry cannot be sustained by domestic resources.

The five year plans required that the agricultural sector produce food and raw materials for the urban population, industry and export, and also that the agricultural sector provide a pool of labor for the mining and manufacturing industries. However, the economic authorities either would not or could not give the agricultural sector much in exchange for its production and labor. The production index for consumer goods remained the same from 1937 through 1942 and declined sharply thereafter, and the volume of consumer goods imports decreased in the 1940's. Thus, the flow of consumer goods to the agricultural sector could only have been increased by depriving the urban sector of these goods. The authorities could make consumer goods less available to some segments of the urban or non-rural population but in no case could the amount of consumer goods for the industrial labor force be reduced since this move would directly affect industrial production. The money wages of the industrial labor force rose but as inflation became more severe, real wages fell and employment in mining and manufacturing had little to offer anyone with an alternate means of livelihood.

The economic authorities never expected the "traditional" or agricultural sector to invest directly in heavy industry, mining or transportation. Instead, Japan and third countries were to provide investment funds and producer goods and the development of these sectors would proceed without requiring the transfer of resources from agriculture to industry. Of the total yen 6.060 billion of planned investment for 1938-1941; Japan was to provide yen 3.030 billion; Manchoukuo, yen

1.690 billion; and third countries, yen 1.330 billion.[1] Thus, the economic
authorities anticipated that Manchoukuo would provide only 28% of investment planned for these sectors.

Initially, the Government had no intention of relying on inflationary
techniques to fulfill the financial investment goals of the first five
year plan. The target for domestic investment was modest and was to be
met through voluntary saving. However, by 1939, it was clear that investment from third countries would be negligible. While actual Japanese
investment amounted roughly to that planned, Manchoukuo sources actually
provided 52% of investment in mining, manufacturing, transportation and
communications, almost double the 28% share planned for domestic investment.

Since it was not possible to raise this amount of domestic investment
through voluntary savings, the Government provided it through the budget.
Revenue from taxes and customs duties was inadequate to cover government
expenditures so the amount of national bonds and loans to the Government
outstanding rose steadily. In fact, in 1937, 1938 and 1939, government
receipts from bond sales and loans exceeded revenues from taxes, customs
duties and monopoly profits. The Central Bank of Manchou assumed the
bulk of national bonds and these bond holdings formed the basis for the
extension of credit and increases in currency circulation. Bank deposits
and currency in circulation increased by 37% in 1937, 62% in 1939, 23%
in 1940, and 35% in 1941.

The increases in currency and deposits inevitably affected the price

---

[1]Tōa Kenkyūjo (Far East Research Institute), Manshūkoku Sangyō Kaihatsu Gokanen Keikaku no Shiryōteki Chōsa Kenkyu, Shikkin Bumon (Study
of the Five Year Plan for Manchurian Industrial Development, Section on
Funds), Tokyo, 1940, p. 21.

level. Prices were controlled but the Government allowed official prices
to rise as inflationary pressures built up though not in proportion to
the increase in currency and deposits. Official prices were undoubtedly
effective for raw materials and the finished products of mining and
manufacturing where the special companies dominated production, but
starting in 1940, a black market in consumer goods flourished in the
cities. Inflation taxed the Manchoukuo population severely after 1938
and the burden was particularly heavy after 1940.

The inflationary financing of investment in Manchurian mining, manufacturing, transportation and communications was effective. During
1938-1942, the growth in inventories and fixed assets in these industries
amounted to yen 6,098 million in current prices, or 87% of the yen 7,007
million in current prices available for investment.

It is more difficult to evaluate the effectiveness of financing
investment through increases in the national debt in maintaining a high
rate of investment in mining, manufacturing, transportation and communications. The estimated rate of domestic investment in these industries
was 14% in 1937, 17% in 1939, and 4% in 1941. The Manchoukuo Government
decided that the 17% rate of domestic investment in 1939 and the undoubtedly high rate in 1940 were excessive and decreased investment sharply
in 1941, when the Industrial Bank of Manchou loans decreased by roughly
yen 300 million and net loans from all sources amounted to only yen 25
million.

The Manchoukuo Government resorted to inflationary techniques of
financing economic development because it was unable to extract savings
from the "traditional" sector through the market mechanism or through
direct controls. But the irony of the situation is that the city-dweller

was more adversely affected by inflation than the farmer who could withdraw from the market and produce for home consumption. The agricultural sector could make this choice because the Government made no attempt to control agricultural production directly and its controls over the distribution of agricultural products were ineffective until 1943.

Inflationary techniques of financing investment may be used effectively in an underdeveloped area, but only up to the point where limitational factors become operative. In the Manchoukuo case, the supply of producer goods from Japan was the limiting factor because by 1941, Japan was the only source of producer goods for Manchurian industrialization. In other underdeveloped countries, the balance of payments and the sociological and political impact of inflation are the likely limiting factors.

APPENDIX I

PRODUCTION INDICES FOR MANUFACTURING IN MANCHOUKUO

Part A: Production Indices by Industry in Manchoukuo, 1936-1944;
1936-1938 Monthly Average as 100

Part B: Production Indices by Commodity in Manchoukuo, 1936-1944;
1936-1938 Monthly Average as 100

These indices were obtained from Mr. S. Hasegawa, a former director
of the Central Bank of Manchou who is now resident in Tokyo. The indices
were based on a survey of manufacturing production made by the Central
Bank of Manchou. The author has never found these indices in published
form and assumes they were not widely distributed.

Unfortunately, little is known about the construction and weighting
of these indices. The production indices by industry are weighted geometric averages of the production of commodities within the particular
industry. No direct indication is given of which commodities are included
in each industry. It appears that the indices by industry are based on
the production indices by commodity which were also compiled by the
Central Bank of Manchou. The base period is the same for both sets of
indices and the production indices for the thirty-four commodities are
arranged in the same order as the production indices compiled by industry
(foodstuffs, paper, textiles, tobacco, etc.). In the case of paper, the
commodity index and the industry index are identical and the production
index for the metals industry corresponds exactly to the production index
for steel products.

According to Mr. Hasegawa, these indices cover the production of
firms employing five or more people.

PART A: PRODUCTION INDICES BY INDUSTRY IN MANCHOUKUO, 1936-1944;
1936-1938 MONTHLY AVERAGE AS 100

INDUSTRY	1936	1937	1938	1939	1940	1941	1942	1943[a]	1944[b]
Foodstuffs	87	109	100	85	90	93	84	52	28
Paper	28	42	98	105	103	101	186	224	163
Textiles	77	100	122	128	114	130	146	156	184
Tobacco	78	102	120	129	128	140	140	138	95
Average for Consumer Goods	81	104	107	100	102	109	105	80	50
Chemicals	23	35	107	138	103	148	174	147	113
Ceramics	64	102	133	185	168	158	202	182	123
Metals	33	86	140	160	170	175	193	222	220
Machinery & Tools	60	86	145	254	252	282	398	366	387
Electricity & Gas	82	96	122	153	171	217	260	292	347
Mining	92	101	107	122	133	153	166	166	156
Forestry	71	121	103	139	249	185	157	137	185
Average for Producer Goods	68	96	114	141	162	171	184	175	178
Average for Manufactures[c]	61	92	118	130	131	142	153	132	108
General Average	71	98	112	129	142	151	158	139	125

[a]Arithmetic average of monthly averages for Jan-Aug., and Dec. (9 months).

[b]Arithmetic average of monthly averages for Jan-June (6 months).

[c]"Average for Manufactures" excludes production of mining and forestry.

The original documents stated that the production relatives were weighted geometric averages. The author believes that the production relatives by year were based on averages computed for each month during the year.

PART B: PRODUCTION INDICES BY COMMODITY IN MANCHOUKUO, 1936-1944;
1936-1938 MONTHLY AVERAGE AS 100

COMMODITY	1936	1937	1938	1939	1940	1941	1942	1943[a]	1944[b]
Flour	93	123	84	50	58	62	75	56	18
Japanese Wine	65	104	131	173	220	261	278	165	301
Beer	50	86	164	215	243	120	269	287	189
Kaolian Wine	95	101	104	119	127	131	58	35	29
Sugar	89	97	114	121	72	96	106	152	107
Chinese Sauce	47	105	148	129	124	143	166	125	96
Japanese Sauce	82	92	126	149	152	157	175	145	126
Paper	28	42	98	105	103	101	186	224	163
Cotton Thread	69	102	128	104	60	72	77	83	124
Cotton Cloth	81	106	113	135	140	156	188	183	209
Wool Cloth	78	94	122	155	184	205	220	278	271
Linen Goods	68	75	148	133	194	221	284	251	231
Cigarettes	78	103	119	126	130	140	141	142	108
Matches	76	85	136	166	108	140	128	106	36
Ammonia Sulphate	94	101	105	91	80	116	144	120	94
Soda Ash	--	85	115	139	166	157	148	153	156
Soy Bean Cake	101	102	97	124	26	74	85	109	102
Bean Oil	91	105	103	123	24	78	83	107	--
Alcohol	67	85	147	166	146	229	220	303	197
Paint	91	85	113	321	477	384	662	348	215
Pulp	--	--	100	111	143	169	170	126	64
Portland Cement	61	103	136	186	154	153	208	238	207
Mixed Cement	63	106	131	163	167	121	129	110	216
Ordinary Bricks	87	100	113	185	260	207	221	160	82
Special Bricks	57	81	162	222	191	214	230	228	245
Steel Products	33	86	140	160	170	175	193	211	225
Pig Iron	78	109	114	136	140	177	229	360	364
Gold	103	107	89	62	65	68	82	288	341
Machinery & Tools	60	86	145	254	252	282	398	342	375
Electricity	82	96	122	151	168	211	254	87	24
Gas	84	92	125	175	220	303	359	247	226
Coal	93	99	108	130	144	165	169	178	190
General Timber	83	122	95	125	264	193	157	126	185
Special Timber	43	116	134	190	209	163			

[a]Arithmetic average of monthly averages for Jan-Aug., and Dec. (9 months).

[b]Arithmetic average of monthly averages for Jan-June (6 months).

Source: Survey by the Central Bank of Manchou. Documents in the possession of Mr. Hasegawa, former director of the Central Bank of Manchou.

APPENDIX II

DATA ON JAPANESE INVESTMENT IN MANCHOUKUO

Part A: Japanese Investment in Manchoukuo Mining, Manufacturing, Transportation and Communications, 1932-1944, as Estimated for Table 16 of Chapter III.

Part B: Northeast China Economic Commission Statistics on Japanese Investment in Manchoukuo 1932-1944

Due to the close economic and political ties between Japan and Manchoukuo it is difficult to trace all Japanese investment in Manchoukuo during the period under study. After careful study of all available data on Japanese investment in Manchoukuo, the author has concluded that the investment statistics compiled by the Northeast China Economic Commission and those published in the Manchoukuo Yearbook, 1942 are the most complete. Furthermore, these series are the only ones compiled on an annual basis in sufficient detail to isolate investment in Manchurian mining, manufacturing, transportation and communications.

Part A presents data on Japanese investment as estimated for Table 16 of Chapter III. Generally speaking, the series published in the Manchoukuo Yearbook, 1942 has been used for the years through 1940, as this series takes repatriation into account although in a few instances it was deemed appropriate to include some data of the Northeast China Economic Commission. The statistics presented in the Northeast China Economic Commission publication are gross figures but they have been used for 1941 through 1944 as no other annual figures are available. Japanese loans to Manchurian firms have been excluded during this period because the statistics for the later years do not take repatriation into account.

The statistics on Japanese investment published by the Northeast China Economic Commission are reproduced in Part B because this series is not available in most libraries.

PART A: JAPANESE INVESTMENT IN MANCHOUKUO MINING, MANUFACTURING, TRANSPORTATION AND COMMUNICATIONS, 1932-1944, AS ESTIMATED FOR TABLE 16 OF CHAPTER III

units: yen 1,000

CATEGORY	1932	1933	1934	1935	1936	1937	1938	1939	1940	1941	1942	1943[a]	1944	TOTAL
BONDS														
Manchuria Heavy Industry Development Co.(Mangyō[5])	-	-	-	-	-	-	-	130,000*	130,000*	145,000	115,000	45,000	-	565,000
Manchuria Coal Mining Co.	-	-	-	-	-	-	-	30,000*	-	-	20,000	-	-	50,000
Pen-hsi-hu Coal and Iron Co.	-	-	-	-	-	-	-	25,000*	20,000*	9,925	-	-	-	54,925
Showa Steel Works	-	-	-	10,000*	18,000*	-	-	70,000*	-	19,887	30,000	10,200	-	157,887
Manchuria Electrical Industry Co.	-	-	-	10,000*	15,000*	-	-	40,000*	60,000*	50,000	50,000	41,700	10,000	276,700
Manchuria Telephone and Telegraph Co.	-	-	8,000*	7,000*	-	8,000*	6,000*	6,000*	14,000*	21,500	21,500	8,000	-	130,000
Manchuria Yalu River Water Power Electric Co.	-	-	-	-	-	-	-	-	20,000	-	30,000	20,000	-	70,000
Manchuria Electric Wire Co.	-	-	-	-	-	-	-	-	-	5,000	5,000	-	-	10,000
South Manchuria Railway Co.	40,000*	20,200*	130,000*	135,000*	155,000*	21,000*	115,000*	210,000*	245,000*	265,000	250,000	270,000	200,000	2,056,200
Manchuria Chemical Co.	-	-	-	-	-	-	10,000*	-	-	2,500	5,000	-	-	17,500
Municipal Communications Co.	-	-	10,000	-	-	-	-	-	5,000	2,500	-	-	-	17,500
South Manchuria Electric Co.	-	-	10,000*	-	-	-	-	-	-	-	-	-	-	10,000
STOCKS RELINQUISHED BY THE JAPANESE GOVERNMENT TO,[b]														
Manchuria Heavy Industry Development Co.(Mangyō[5])	-	-	-	-	-	-	-	20,500	63,900	54,800	-	-	-	139,200
Manchuria Mining Development Co.	-	-	-	-	17,724	-	3,444	25,710	4,035	30,983	-	-	-	81,896
Manchuria Electrical Industry Co.	-	-	-	-	-	-	-	-	750	-	-	-	-	750

CATEGORY	1932	1933	1934	1935	1936	1937	1938	1939	1940	1941	1942	1943ᵃ	1944	TOTAL
CORPORATE STOCK														
Manchuria Carbon Industry Co.	-	-	-	-	-	-	-	-	-	-	-	-	5,000	5,000
Continental Chemical Industry Co.	-	-	-	-	-	-	-	-	-	-	-	-	5,000	5,000
Pen-hsi-hu Coal and Iron Co.	-	-	-	2,500	-	-	-	-	-	40,000	-	-	-	42,500
Manchuria Electrical Industry Co.	-	-	-	-	-	1,724	-	2,084	8,339	21,601	24,000	23,225	29,560	110,533
Manchuria Telephone and Telegraph Co.	-	3,814	-	-	4,430	-	-	4,446	7,894	7,998	5,596	5,785	5,875	45,838
Manchuria Yalu River Water Power Co.	-	-	-	-	-	6,250	6,250	12,500	-	6,250	-	6,250	-	37,500
Manchuria Electric Wire Co.	-	-	-	-	-	3,750	1,250	2,500	2,500	2,500	-	5,000	7,500	25,000
Manchuria Ichikawajima Machine Factory	-	-	-	-	-	-	-	-	-	-	-	-	5,000	5,000
Manchuria Electro-Chemical Co.	-	-	-	-	-	-	-	-	1,500	375	-	-	-	1,875
Nan-piao Coal Mining Co.	-	-	-	-	-	-	-	-	-	-	-	-	4,000	4,000
Hi-shan Coal Mining Co.	-	-	-	-	-	-	-	10,000	-	25,000	50,000	25,000	-	100,000
Manchuria Shale Oil Co.	-	-	-	-	-	-	-	-	22,500	24,000	12,000	16,000	8,750	93,250
Bo-sheng Liquid Fuel Co.	-	-	-	-	-	3,400	-	4,400	10,800	5,400	-	6,600	6,600	37,200
South Manchuria Railway Co.	25,000*	61,000*	36,000*	36,000*	36,000*	56,000*	20,000*	40,000*	100,000*	80,000	110,000	106,558	160,489	867,047
Manchuria Chemical Industry Co.	-	5,050	-	-	2,547	-	2,649	-	-	-	-	-	-	10,246
South Manchuria Gas Co.	-	-	-	-	-	-	-	-	1,597	-	-	-	-	1,597
Antung Light Metals Co.	-	-	-	-	-	-	-	-	-	-	-	-	25,000	25,000

CATEGORY	1932	1923	1924	1925	1926	1927	1928	1929	1940	1941	1942	1943[a]	1944	TOTAL
CORPORATE STOCK cont'd[d]														
Manchuria Kobe Metals Co.	–	–	–	–	–	–	–	–	–	–	–	–	10,000	10,000
South Manchuria Mining Co.	–	–	–	–	–	–	–	–	–	–	–	–	5,636	5,636
Dairen Machine Manufacturing Co.	–	–	–	–	–	–	–	–	–	–	–	3,332	8,691	12,023
Lead Mining Co.	–	–	–	–	–	–	–	–	–	–	–	5,000	–	5,000
Manchuria Heavy Industry Development Co. (Mangyo)	–	–	–	–	–	–	–	27,135	28,742	–	55,000	–	–	110,877
CAPITAL FOR UNPROFITABLE CO'S[c]	–	–	–	–	–	–	–	–	–	–	–	–	101,242	101,242
LOANS AND OTHERS[d]														
Manchuria Heavy Industry Development Co. (Mangyo)[ō]	–	–	–	–	–	10,000*	38,500*	20,000*	–28,000*	–	–	–	–	40,500*
South Manchuria Railway Co.	–	–	–	75,000*	–75,300*	84,000*	–59,000*	25,000*	–5,000*	–	–	–	–	45,000*
Manchuria Chemical Industry Co.	–	–	12,000*	–	–6,250*	4,050*	–9,800*	–	–	–	–	–	–	000[a]
Manchuria Electrical Industry Co.	–	–	–	–	–	–	20,000*	15,000*	–10,000*	–	–	–	–	25,000*
Manchuria Coal Mining Co.	–	–	–	5,000*	5,000*	10,000*	10,000*	–	–	–	–	–	–	30,000*
Pen-hsi-hu Coal and Iron Co.	–	–	–	–	–	–	–	4,000*	15,000*	–	–	–	–	19,000*
North Manchuria Railway Co.	–	–	–	60,000*	60,000*	60,000*	50,000*	–	–	–	–	–	–	230,000*
Hydro-Electric Power Loan	–	–	–	–	–	–	–	50,000*	–	–	–	–	–	50,000*
Opening of South Manchuria R.R. Holding Shares[c]	–	–	–	340*	17,205*	–	1,344*	15,391*	3,950*	–	–	–	–	38,230*
TOTAL INVESTMENT	65,000	90,064	206,000	350,840	249,656	268,174	225,637	789,666	702,507	820,219	783,096	597,450	598,343	5,746,652

aData refer to the period April 1, 1943 through March of the following year.

b"Stocks Relinquished by the Japanese Government to:" This category is nowhere explained. The author believes it refers to stock held by the Japanese Government which was transferred to the firm in question.

c"Capital for Unprofitable Companies": This item is likewise not explained. This item must represent subsidies paid to firms suffering losses.

dThe data on loans for 1941-1944 have been excluded because the statistics did not take repayment into account.

Sources:

Data marked with an (*): Manchoukuo Yearbook, 1942, op. cit., pp. 290-291.

All other data: Northeast China Economic Commission, op. cit., XIX, Appendix 2, pp. 200-227.

PART B: NORTHEAST CHINA ECONOMIC COMMISSION STATISTICS ON JAPANESE INVESTMENT IN MANCHOUKUO, 1932-1944

"Yearly Comparison of Actual Investments By Japan in Manchuria"

CATEGORY	1932	1933	1934	1935	1936	1937	1938	1939	1940	1941	1942	1943[a]	1944	TOTAL
BONDS														
Government Bonds	60,000 20,000	26,900 30,000	178,850 10,000	324,400 75,400	157,510 44,600	231,360 83,360	343,590 111,640	256,912 65,300	296,500 215,000	501,312 240,000	761,500 110,000	516,700 20,000	277,000 -	5,384,534 1,045,000
Manchuria Reclamation Co.	-	-	-	-	-	-	30,000	73,000	30,000	100,000	95,000	77,000	50,000	455,000
Manchuria Heavy Industry Development Co. (Mangyo)	-	-	-	-	-	-	30,000	150,000	90,000	145,000	115,000	45,000	-	575,000
Manchuria Coal Mining Co.	-	-	-	10,000	-	10,000	19,950	39,850	-	-	-	-	-	79,800
Pen-hsi-hu Coal and Iron Co.	-	-	-	-	-	-	-	24,937	15,000	9,925	20,000	-	-	69,862
Showa Steel Works	-	-	-	10,000	12,910	-	-	69,825	-	19,887	30,000	10,000	-	157,622
Manchuria Electrial Industry Co.	-	-	-	10,000	15,000	-	20,000	55,000	50,000	50,000	50,000	41,700	10,000	301,700
Industrial Bank	-	-	-	-	-	-	10,000	20,000	55,000	40,000	30,000	25,000	10,000	190,000
Telephone and Telegraph Co.	-	-	8,000	7,000	-	8,000	6,000	6,000	14,000	21,500	21,500	8,000	-	100,000
Manchuria Yalu River Water Power Electric Co.	-	-	-	-	-	-	-	-	20,000	-	30,000	20,000	-	70,000
Manchuria Electric Wire Co.	-	-	-	-	-	-	-	-	-	5,000	5,000	-	-	10,000
South Manchuria Railway Co.	40,000	39,700	140,000	210,000	80,000	130,000	106,000	230,000	300,000	265,000	250,000	270,000	200,000	2,260,700
Manchuria Chemical Co.	-	-	-	-	-	-	10,000	-	2,500	2,500	5,000	-	-	20,000
Municipal Communications Co.	-	-	10,000	-	-	-	-	-	5,000	2,500	-	-	-	17,500
Other	-	9,200	10,850	2,000	-	-	-	3,300	-	-	-	-	7,000	32,350

CATEGORY	1932	1933	1934	1935	1936	1937	1938	1939	1940	1941	1942	1943[a]	1944	TOTAL
STOCKS RELINQUISHED BY THE JAPANESE GOVERNMENT TO:														
Manchurian Government	–	–	–	–	17,724	–	3,444	64,748	68,685	100,783	–	–	–	255,384
	–	–	–	–	–	–	–	–	–	15,000	–	–	–	15,000
Manchuria Heavy Industry Development Co. (Mangyo)	–	–	–	–	–	–	–	20,500	63,900	54,800	–	–	–	139,200
Manchuria Mining Development Co.	–	–	–	–	17,724	–	3,444	25,710	4,035	30,983	–	–	–	81,896
Industrial Bank	–	–	–	–	–	–	–	18,533	–	–	–	–	–	18,538
Manchuria Electrical Industry Co.	–	–	–	–	–	–	–	–	750	–	–	–	–	750
CORPORATE STOCK	25,000	69,864	36,000	38,500	50,477	66,124	58,424	84,280	166,380	216,874	260,346	210,875	426,133	1,729,272
Manchuria Reclamation Co.	–	–	–	–	–	15,000	1,650	8,350	3,750	3,750	3,750	8,125	8,125	52,500
Manchuria Carbon Industry Co.	–	–	–	–	–	–	–	–	–	–	–	–	5,000	5,000
Continental Chemical Industry Co.	–	–	–	–	–	–	–	–	–	–	–	–	5,000	5,000
Pen-hsi-hu Coal and Iron Co.	–	–	–	2,500	–	–	–	–	–	40,000	–	–	–	42,500
Manchuria Electrical Industry Co.	–	–	–	–	–	1,724	–	2,084	8,339	21,601	24,000	23,225	29,560	110,533
Industrial Bank	–	–	–	–	7,500	–	–	–	7,500	–	–	–	1,687	16,687
Manchuria Telephone and Telegraph Co.	–	3,814	–	–	4,430	–	–	4,446	7,894	7,996	5,596	5,785	5,875	45,838
Toyo Reclamation Co.	–	–	–	–	–	–	–	–	–	–	–	–	9,000	9,000

CATEGORY	1932	1933	1934	1935	1936	1937	1938	1939	1940	1941	1942	1943[a]	1944	TOTAL
CORPORATE STOCK, cont'd.														
Manchuria Yalu River Water Power Electric Co.	-	-	-	-	-	6,250	6,250	12,500	-	6,250	-	6,250	-	37,500
Manchuria Electric Wire Co.	-	-	-	-	-	3,750	1,250	2,500	2,500	2,500	-	5,000	7,500	25,000
Manchuria Ishikawajima Machine Factory	-	-	-	-	-	-	-	-	-	-	-	-	5,000	5,000
Manchuria Electro-Chemical Co.	-	-	-	-	-	-	-	-	1,500	375	-	-	-	1,875
Nan-piao Coal Mining Co.	-	-	-	-	-	-	-	-	-	-	-	-	4,300	4,300
Mi-shan Coal Mining Co.	-	-	-	-	-	-	-	-	-	25,000	50,000	25,000	-	100,000
Manchuria Shale Oil Co.	-	-	-	-	-	-	-	10,000	22,500	24,000	12,000	16,000	8,750	93,250
Ho-ch'eng Liquid Fuel Co.	-	-	-	-	-	3,400	-	4,400	10,800	5,400	-	6,600	6,600	37,200
South Manchuria Railway Co.	25,000	61,000	36,000	36,000	36,000	56,000	20,000	40,000	100,000	80,000	110,000	106,558	160,489	867,047
Manchuria Chemical Industry Co.	-	5,050	-	-	2,547	-	2,649	-	-	-	-	-	-	10,246
South Manchuria Gas Co.	-	-	-	-	-	-	-	-	1,597	-	-	-	-	1,597
Antung Light Metals Co.	-	-	-	-	-	-	-	-	-	-	-	-	25,000	25,000
Manchuria Kobe Metals Co.	-	-	-	-	-	-	-	-	-	-	-	-	10,000	10,000
South Manchuria Mining Co.	-	-	-	-	-	-	-	-	-	-	-	-	5,636	5,636
Dairen Machine Manufacturing Co.	-	-	-	-	-	-	-	-	-	-	-	3,332	8,691	12,023
Lead Mining Co.	-	-	-	-	-	-	-	-	-	-	-	5,000	-	5,000
Manchuria Heavy Industry Development Co. (Mangyō)	-	-	-	-	-	-	26,625	-	-	-	55,000	-	-	81,625
Other Companies	-	-	-	-	-	-	-	-	-	-	-	-	120,220	120,220

CATEGORY	192.	1933	1934	193.	1936	1937	193.	1939	1940	1941	1942	1943[a]	1944	TOTAL
CAPITAL FOR UNPROFITABLE CO'S														
Electro-Chemical Co.	-	-	-	-	-	-	-	-	-	-	-	-	101,242 / 16,400	101,242 / 16,400
Manchuria Chemical Industry Co.	-	-	-	-	-	-	-	-	-	-	-	-	11,787	11,787
Manchuria Soda Co.	-	-	-	-	-	-	-	-	-	-	-	-	15,726	15,726
Kobe Metals Co.	-	-	-	-	-	-	-	-	-	-	-	-	4,969	4,969
Mitsubishi Kwantung Ling-ku-t'u Co.	-	-	-	-	-	-	-	-	-	-	-	-	31,582	31,582
Dairen Wharf Co.	-	-	-	-	-	-	-	-	-	-	-	-	15,010	15,010
Honen Oil Co.	-	-	-	-	-	-	-	-	-	-	-	-	4,768	4,768
LOANS AND OTHERS	12,203	11,765	32,335	19,275	37,966	135,552	119,047	160,421	133,924	205,519	277,420	262,169	116,179	1,598,675
Manchuria Reclamation Co.	-	-	-	-	-	5,000	-	-	-	-	-	-	-	5,000
Manchuria Heavy Industry Development Co. (Mangyo)	-	-	-	-	-	-	-	-	3,355	4,150	-	-	-	7,505
Showa Steel Works	-	-	-	-	-	-	-	2,900	-	-	-	-	-	2,900
Manchuria Yalu River Water Power Electric Co.	-	-	-	-	-	1,937	12,455	18,602	10,586	11,334	-	-	-	54,914
Industrial Bank	-	-	-	-	-	25,000	-	-	-	7,000	-	-	-	32,000
Manchuria Shale Oil Co.	-	-	-	-	-	-	-	-	-	23,145	-	-	-	23,145
Ho-ch'eng Liquid Fuel Co.	-	-	-	-	-	-	-	-	-	5,000	3,000	-	-	8,000
South Manchuria Railway Co.	-	-	-	-	-	30,000	15,000	50,000	40,350	-	-	-	-	135,350
Manchuria Chemical Industry Co.	-	-	10,800	1,500	-	1,400	-	1,100	-	-	-	-	-	14,800
Municipal Communications Co.	-	-	-	-	-	-	1,000	-	-	-	2,500	-	-	3,500
Ta-ch'an Mining Co.	-	-	-	-	-	-	-	-	-	-	-	1,016	-	1,016

CATEGORY	1932	1933	1934	1935	1936	1937	1938	1939	1940	1941	1942	1943[a]	1944	TOTAL
LOANS AND OTHERS, cont'd														
South Manchuria Mining Co.	-	-	-	-	-	-	-	-	-	-	-	2,500	-	2,500
Manchuria Soda Co.	-	-	-	-	-	-	-	-	-	-	-	-	6,000	6,000
Manchuria Electrical Industry Co.	-	-	-	-	-	-	-	-	-	-	-	-	2,000	2,000
Fushun Coal Mining Co.	-	-	-	-	-	-	-	-	-	-	-	1,900	1,740	3,640
South Manchuria Gas Co.	-	-	-	-	-	-	-	-	-	-	-	1,680	-	1,680
Reserve Capital of Electro Chemical Industry Co.	-	-	-	-	-	-	-	-	-	-	-	5,900	-	5,900
Fixed Assets Co.	-	-	-	-	-	-	-	-	-	-	-	3,332	-	3,332
Manchuria Hitachi Manufacturing Co.	-	-	-	-	-	-	-	-	-	-	-	-	1,193	1,193
Manchuria Mongolia Wool Textile Co.	-	-	-	-	-	-	-	-	-	-	-	-	1,732	1,732
Others	12,203	11,765	17,775	37,966	72,215	91,492	96,819	139,633	154,890	271,920[b]	237,841[c]	111,514[d]	1,282,568
GRAND TOTAL	97,203	160,529	252,185	382,175	263,677	453,036	525,405	1,075,361	1,225,489	1,421,488	1,299,266	985,744	920,554	9,069,112

"Amount redeemed not included". The author assumes that this means repatriation is not included and therefore the figures represent gross Japanese investment in Manchoukuo. If this is the case, the figures on loans overstate this form of Japanese investment in Manchoukuo throughout the period. Repatriation of Japanese investment in corporate shares and debentures was probably negligible until 1941.

[a]1943 data refer to the period April 1, 1943 through March of the following year.

[b]Includes housing capital for the Manchuria Reclamation Company.

[c]Amount not yet paid in: 932,000 yuan.

[d]Agricultural land development outside the designated sphere is included in that of the Manchuria Reclamation Company.

Source: Northeast China Economic Commission, op. cit., XIX, Appendix 1, pp. 200 - 227.

BIBLIOGRAPHY

ENGLISH LANGUAGE MATERIALS

Books

Bank of Korea. Economic History of Manchuria. Seoul, 1920.

Borton, Hugh. Japan's Modern Century. New York: Ronald Press, 1955.

Cohen, Jerome B. Japan's Economy in War and Reconstruction.
Institute of Pacific Relations. Minneapolis: University of Minnesota
Press, 1949.

Dull, Paul S. and Umemura, Michael Takaaki. The Tokyo Trials.
(Center for Japanese Studies, Occasional Papers No. 6.)
Ann Arbor: The University of Michigan Press, 1956.

Japan Economic Federation. Foreign Relations Council. The Currency and
Finance of Manchoukuo. (East Asia Economic Intelligence Series,
No. 7.) Tokyo, 1940.

Jones, Francis C. Manchuria Since 1931. London: Royal Institute of
International Affairs, 1949.

Kuznets, Simon. Commodity Flow and Capital Formation. Vol. I. New York:
National Bureau of Economic Research, 1938.

Kuznets, Simon. National Product Since 1869. (National Bureau of Economic
Research, Publication No. 46.) New York: National Bureau of Economic
Research, 1946.

Lange, Oscar and Taylor, Fred. M. On the Economic Theory of Socialism.
Edited by B. E. Lippencott. Minneapolis: University of Minnesota
Press, 1938.

Library of Congress. Reference Department. Manchuria, an Annotated
Bibliography. Compiled by Peter A. Berton. Washington, 1951.

The Manchoukuo Yearbook Company. The Manchoukuo Yearbook, 1942.
Hsinking, 1942.

Pauley, Edwin W. Report on Japanese Assets in Manchuria to the President
of the United States, July 1946. Washington: U. S. Government
Printing Office, 1946.

Schumpeter, Elizabeth B. (ed.) The Industrialization of Japan and
Manchoukuo, 1930-1940. New York: Macmillan Co., 1940.

South Manchuria Railway Company. Report on Progress in Manchuria, 1907-1928. Dairen, 1929.

_____. 2nd. Report on Progress in Manchuria to 1930. Dairen, 1930.

_____. 3rd. Report on Progress in Manchuria to 1932. Dairen, 1932.

_____. 4th. Report on Progress in Manchuria to 1934. Dairen, 1934.

_____. 5th. Report on Progress in Manchuria to 1936. Dairen, 1936.

_____. 6th. Report on Progress in Manchuria to 1939. Dairen, 1939.

United Nations. Department of Economic Affairs. Budgetary Structure and Classification of Government Accounts. New York, 1951.

U.S. Bureau of the Census. The Population of Manchuria. By Waller Wynne, Jr. (International Population Statistics Reports, Series P-90, No. 7.) Washington: U.S. Government Printing Office, 1958.

Articles and Periodicals

Bergson, Abram. "Soviet National Income and Product in 1937," Quarterly Journal of Economics. Part I: May, 1950. Part II: August, 1950.

Bisson, T.A. "Soviet-Japanese Relations, 1931-1938," Foreign Policy Reports, XIV, No. 22 (Feb. 1, 1939). New York: Foreign Policy Association, pp. 258-272.

Boody, Elizabeth. "Manchoukuo, the Key to Japan's Foreign Exchange Problem," Far Eastern Survey, VI, No. 10 (May 12, 1937), 107-112.

Friedman, Milton. "Discussion of the Inflationary Gap," Essays in Positive Economics. Chicago: University of Chicago Press, 1953. 251-262.

Hamilton, Earl J. "Profit Inflation and the Industrial Revolution, 1751-1800," Quarterly Journal of Economics, LVI, No. 2 (February, 1942), 256-73.

"Heavy Industry in Manchoukuo," Oriental Economist, XII, No. 2 (February 1945), 71-74.

Institute of Pacific Relations. American Council. Far Eastern Survey. Fortnightly Research Service. 1932-1946.

"Japanese Investment in Manchuria," Contemporary Manchuria, III, No. 1 (January, 1939), 1-18.

"Japan's Manchoukuo Investments," <u>Oriental Economist</u>, VII, No. 3 (March, 1940), 152-154.

"The Manchoukuo-German Trade Agreement," <u>Contemporary Manchuria</u>, I, No. 3 (September, 1937), 33-47.

Reubens, Edwin P. "Opportunities, Governments and Economic Development in Manchuria, 1860-1940," <u>The State and Economic Growth</u>. New York: Social Science Research Council, 1956.

South Manchuria Railway Company. <u>Contemporary Manchuria</u>. Vols. I - V. Dairen, 1937-1941.

Stewart, John R. "Foreign Investments in Manchuria," <u>Far Eastern Survey</u>, IV, No. 11 (June 5, 1935), 81-35.

_____. "Manchurian Heavy Industry Reorganized," <u>Far Eastern Survey</u>, X, No. 8 (September 8, 1941).

Tokyo Keizai Simposha. <u>The Oriental Economist</u>. Vols. I - XII. Tokyo, 1934-1945.

Unpublished Materials

Meyers, Ramon. "The Japanese Economic Development of Manchuria." Unpublished Ph. D. dissertation, University of Washington, 1959.

Northeast China Economic Commission. <u>Economic Encyclopedia of the Northeast</u>. Vol. I-A: Resources and Industry of Northeast China. Vol. I-B: Resources and Industry of Northeast China. Vol. III: Distribution of Farm Products in Northeast China. Vol. XII: The Cement Industry in Northeast China. Vol. XIII: Paper Pulp Industry in Northeast China. Vol. XIV: The Textile Industry in Northeast China. Vol. XV: Transportation in Northeast China. Vol. XIX: Money and Banking in Northeast China. Vol. XX: Trade. Mukden, 1947-1948. (Mimeographed.)
    These volumes are translations made by a U.S. Government agency of a series written in Chinese. This series was written in Mukden during 1947 and 1948 on the basis of information gathered from Japanese who had been active in economic affairs. The Chinese title of the series is <u>Tung-pei Ching-chi Hsiao-ts'ung-shu</u>. The series published in Chinese consisted of twenty volumes.

Wald, Royal Jules. "The Young Officer Movement in Japan, 1925-1937: Ideology and Actions." Unpublished Ph. D. dissertation, University of California at Berkely, 1949.

JAPANESE LANGUAGE MATERIALS

Books

Dairen Shōkō Kaigisho (Dairen Chamber of Commerce). Manshū Ginkō Kaisha Nenkan (Yearbook of Manchurian Banks and Companies). Annual. Dairen, 1935-1942.

_____. Manshū Jigyō Seiseki Bunseki (Analysis of the Business Results of Manchurian Enterprises). 5 vols. Dairen, 1937-1941.

_____. Manshū Keizai Tōkei Nenpō (Yearbook of Manchurian Economic Statistics). Annual. Dairen, 1927-1941.

Fujiwara, Yutaka. Manshūkoku Tōsei Keizai-ron (The Manchoukuo Scheme of Economic Controls). Tokyo: Nihon Hyōronsha, 1942.

Kikuchi, Chikara. Manshū Jūyō Sangyō no Kōsei: Manshu Tokushu Kaisha no Bunseki (The Composition of Manchurian Heavy Industry: A Study of Special Companies in Manchuria). Hsinking: Tōyō Keizai Shuppan, 1939.

Kokumin Keizai Kenkyū Kyōkai. Kinzoku Kōgyō Chōsakai (National Association for Economic Studies, Metals Industry Survey Association). Daiichiji Manshū Sangyō Kaihatsu Gokanen Keikakusho (The First Five Year Plan for Manchurian Industrial Development). Tokyo, 1946.

Manshū Jūkōgyō Kaihatsu Kaisha (Manchuria Heavy Industries Development Company). Mangyō narabi Zaiman Kankei Dōsha Jigyō Gaiyō (An Outline of Mangyō and Its Subsidiaries in Manchoukuo). Mukden, 1939.

Mammō Dōhō Engokai (Manchuria-Mongolian Fraternal Relief Society). Manshūkokushi Hensan Shiryō, Sono Ichi Tosho Mokuroku (Materials for the Compilation of Manchoukuo History and Their Bibliography). Tokyo, 1956.

Manshū Chōsa Kikai Rengōkai (Institute for Manchoukuo Studies). Manshūkoku Kokumin Shotoku Chōsasho (A Study of Manchoukuo National Income). 2 vols. Hsinking, 1943.

Manshū Chūō Ginkō (Central Bank of Manchou). Kinyū Keizai Tōkei Nenpō (Yearbook of Financial Statistics). Annual. Hsinking, 1935-1943.

_____. Manshū Bukka Chōsa (Survey of Manchurian Prices). Annual. Hsinking, 1939-1943.

_____. Manshū Bukka Rōgin Shirabe (An Investigation of Manchurian Prices and Wages). Hsinking, 1939.

Manshū Chūō Ginkō (Central Bank of Manchou). Manshū Chūō Ginkō Jūnenshi (Ten Year History of the Central Bank of Manchou). Hsinking, 1942.

_____. Manshū Kinyū Sankō Tōkei (Reference Statistics for Manchurian Finances). Hsinking, 1943.

_____. Manshū Oroshiuri Bukka Nenpō (Yearbook of Manchurian Wholesale Prices). Annual. Hsinking, 1936-1939.

Manshū Kōgyō Ginkō (Industrial Bank of Manchou). Manshū Jigyō Kaisha Seiseki Bunseki (Analysis of the Business Results of Manchurian Enterprises). Annual. Hsinking, 1941, 1942.

_____. Manshū Tōsei Keizai ni tsuite (Economic Controls in Manchuria). Hsinking, 1941.

_____. Tokushu narabi ni Juntokushu Kaisha Shirabe A Survey of Special and Semi-special Companies). Hsinking, 1941.

_____. Yokin Tsūka yori mitaru Manshū no Shinyō Keizai (Deposits, Currency and Credit in the Manchurian Economy). Hsinking, 1939.

Manshū Kōkō Gijutsu-in Kyōkai (Association of Technicians in Manchurian Mining and Manufacturing). Manshū Kōkō Nenkan (Manchurian Mining and Manufacturing Yearbook). Tokyo, 1942.

Manshūkoku. Keizaibu (Manchoukuo. Economic Affairs Section). Kouri Bukka Tōkei Nenpō (Statistical Yearbook for Retail Prices). Annual. Hsinking, 1934-1940.

_____. Oroshiuri Bukka Tōkei Nenpō (Yearbook of Wholesale Price Statistics). Annual, Hsinking, 1934-1941.

_____. Tōsei Kakaku Hinmoku Benran (Manual of Price Control Commodities). Hsinking, 1943.

Manshūkoku. Sangyōbu (Manchoukuo. Production Section). Manshūkoku Kōjō Tōkei (Manchoukuo Factory Statistics). Annual. Hsinking, 1936-1940.

Manshūkoku. Sōmuchō (Manchoukuo. General Affairs Board). Manshū Keizai Sankō Shiryō (Manchurian Economic Reference Materials). Hsinking, 1939.

_____. Manshūkoku Yosan (Manchoukuo Budget Estimates). Annual. Hsinking, 1934-1940.

Manshūkoku. Zaiseibu (Manchoukuo. Department of Finance). Manshūkoku Gaikoku Bōeki Nenpō (Statistical Yearbook of the Foreign Trade of Manchoukuo). Annual. Hsinking, 1934-1940.

Minami Manshū Tetsudō (South Manchuria Railway). Manshū Dochaku Shihon Jittai Chōsa Hōkokusho (Report on a Survey of Native Capital in Manchuria). 2 vols. Dairen, 1942.

_____. Manshū Gokanen Keikaku Gaiyō (Outline of the Manchurian Five Year Plan). Dairen, 1937.

_____. Manshū Infureshon Chōsa Hōkoku (Report on an Investigation of Inflation in Manchuria). Dairen, 1941.

_____. Manshū Kaisha Kōkahyō Shūsei, Kōgyōhen (Compilation of the Business Records of Manchurian Companies, Manufacturing). Dairen, 1936.

_____. Manshū Keizai Kenkyū Nenpō (Yearbook of Manchurian Economic Studies). Tokyo, 1937-1941.

_____. Manshū Keizai Nenpō (Manchou Economic Yearbook). Tokyo: Kaizosha, 1933-1941.

_____. Manshū Keizai Tōkei Nenpō (Yearbook of Manchou Economic Statistics). Annual. Dairen, 1927-1939.

_____. Manshū ni okeru Bukka Chōsa narabi ni Shisū Kōsei no Genjō (Manchurian Price Studies and the Construction of Price Indices). Dairen, 1941.

_____. Manshū ni okeru Sankeihi Shisū no Jissai (Cost of Living Indices in Manchuria). Dairen, 1939.

_____. Manshū Sangyō Tōkei (Manchurian Production Statistics). Annual. Dairen.

_____. Manshū Tōsei Keizai Shiryō (Materials on Manchurian Economic Controls). Dairen, 1939.

_____. Manshūkoku Gaikoku Bōeki Shōsai Tōkei (Manchoukuo Foreign Trade Statistics). Annual. Dairen, 1924-1939.

Ōkurashō. Kanrikyoku (Japanese Ministry of Finance. Administrative Division). Nihonjin Kaigai Katsudō ni Kansuru Rekishiteki Chōsa. Manshū hen. Daisanbu: Manshū no Keizai (A Historical Investigation of the Overseas Activity of Japanese. Section on Manchuria. Part III: The Economy of Manchuria). Tokyo, 1947.

Tōyō Keizai (Oriental Economist). Kabushiki Kaisha Nenkan (Yearbook of Stock Companies). No. 16. Tokyo, 1938.

Sakairi, Chotarō. Manshū Sangyō Haibun Ron (The Distribution of Manchurian Industry). Tokyo, 1944.

Shōken Hikeuke Kaisha Tōseikai (Control Association for Stock Companies). Kabushiki Kaisha Nenpō (Yearbook of Stock Companies). Tokyo, 1944.

Tōa Kenkyūjo (Far East Research Institute). Manshūkoku Sangyō Kaihatsu Goksnen Keikaku no Shiryōteki Chōsa Kenkyū, Shikkin Bumon (Study of the Five Year Plan for Manchurian Industrial Development, Section on Funds). Tokyo, 1940.

Watanabe, Takeshi. Manshū Keizai no Shindōkō (Recent Trends of the Manchurian Economy). Tokyo, 1943.

Articles and Periodicals

Adachi, Yoshinobu. "Manshū Kōgyō Rōdō ni Kan suru futatsu mitsu no Kōsatsu," (Two or three Case Studies of Labor in Manchurian Manufacturing), Mantetsu Chōsa Geppō (South Manchuria Railway Monthly Studies). Dairen, 1940.

Kurazono, Susumu. "Tenkanki no Manshūkoku Zaisei," (Manchoukuo Public Finance at a Turning Point), Manshū Keizai Kenkyū Nenpō (Yearbook of Manchurian Economic Studies). Tokyo: South Manchuria Railway Company, 1941, 401-432.

Manshū Chūō Ginkō (Central Bank of Manchou). Manshū Kinyū Keizai Geppō (Monthly of Manchurian Finance). Monthly. Hsinking.

Manshūkoku. Keizaibu (Manchoukuo. Economic Affairs Section). Keizaibu Tōkei Geppō (Statistical Monthly of the Economic Affairs Section). Monthly. Hsinking, 1935-1941.

Minami Manshū Tetsudō (South Manchuria Railway). Manshū Keizai Tōkei Kihō (Quarterly of Manchou Economic Statistics). No. 1 (November, 1941). No. 2 (March, 1942). No. 3 (August, 1943). Hsinking.

_____. Mantetsu Chōsa Geppō (South Manchuria Railway Monthly Studies). Monthly. Dairen, 1933-1943.

Sataru, Yoshio. "Senjitaiseika no Manjin Rōdōsha no Jōtai," (Wartime Conditions of Manchurian Labor). Manshū Keizai Kenkyū Nenpō (Yearbook of Manchurian Economic Studies). Tokyo: South Manchuria Railway Company, 1940, 360-372.

Shuzui, Hajime. "Dochaku Shihon to Shikkin Dōin," (Native Capital and the Mobilization of Funds), Manshū Keizai Kenkyū Nenpo (Yearbook of Manchurian Economic Studies). Tokyo: South Manchuria Railway Company, 1941, 291-353.

Other Sources

Suitsu Document Collection. Hitotsubashi Daigaku. Keizai Kenkyūjo (Hitotsubashi University. Economic Research Institute). Uncatalogued.

For Product Safety Concerns and Information please contact our EU
representative GPSR@taylorandfrancis.com
Taylor & Francis Verlag GmbH, Kaufingerstraße 24, 80331 München, Germany

www.ingramcontent.com/pod-product-compliance
Lightning Source LLC
Chambersburg PA
CBHW070731270326
41926CB00068B/2999

9 781138 369146